GODS AND GODDESSES IN
Art and Legend

GODS AND GODDESSES
IN
Art and Legend

BY

HERMAN J. WECHSLER

GREAT MYTHS
AS PICTURED BY
GREAT MASTERS

WASHINGTON SQUARE PRESS, INC. • NEW YORK

GODS AND GODDESSES IN ART AND LEGEND

1961

The illustrations in this book are printed from new engraved cylinders made specially for this edition.

Designed by Maxwell Marxe

L

Published by
Washington Square Press, Inc.: Executive Offices, 630 Fifth Avenue;
University Press Division, 32 Washington Place, New York, N.Y.

WASHINGTON SQUARE PRESS editions are distributed in the U.S. by
Affiliated Publishers, Inc., 630 Fifth Avenue, New York 20, N.Y.

ACKNOWLEDGMENTS

I wish to acknowledge with gratitude the cooperation of the following institutions which have permitted the reproduction of paintings in their collections:

THE ISABELLA STEWART GARDNER MUSEUM, Boston, Mass.
YALE UNIVERSITY ART GALLERY, New Haven, Conn.
NATIONAL GALLERY OF ART, Washington, D. C.
THE METROPOLITAN MUSEUM OF ART, New York
NATIONAL GALLERY, London, England

I owe a special debt to ERICH S. HERRMANN for having secured from abroad the necessary photographs of paintings in foreign collections.

DAVID ASHLEY, INC., of New York has generously permitted reproduction of the fine color fascsimile of Botticelli's *The Birth of Venus* which appears on the front cover.

Lastly I wish to express appreciation for the courtesy and help of COLONEL H. A. McBRIDE of the National Gallery of Art, Washington, D. C. Through his efforts special color separations have been furnished for the details of the paintings reproduced on the back and inner covers of this book: *The Feast of the Gods*, Giovanni Bellini; *Venus and Adonis*, Titian; *Circe and Her Lovers*, Dosso Dossi.

HERMAN J. WECHSLER

CONTENTS

LIST OF ILLUSTRATIONS

LIST OF ILLUSTRATIONS—Cont.

THE IDEA for this volume arose out of an experience which dates back a good many years, to that time in fact when, as a young student, I first began to seek out paintings by the great masters in those far-flung places where they were enshrined.

Time and again I discovered, when standing before a well-known work of art, that I felt thwarted and dissatisfied. It was all very fine to stare at Danaë, as represented by Titian or Tintoretto; or Icarus, falling through the skies; or Venus, floating shoreward on a huge sea shell. Yet I wished, as I stood in some museum corridor, or in the vastness of an Italian palace, or in the ancient city of Pompeii, that I knew more of the details of the stories, as represented on panels or canvases or frescoed walls. Some of them I recalled vaguely, for, like most schoolboys, I had been exposed to Homer's *Odyssey* and *Iliad*. But time had dimmed these tales in my memory, and I discovered that in this I was not alone. There were others who felt, as I did, that many paintings by the masters, in which the great legends were pictured, would take on a greater significance if memories could be refreshed.

This book, then, will be a kind of sampler or "introduction to mythology," to use a schoolroom phrase. But since myths and legends are in reality stories of long ago, this is primarily a "story book" and the reader may look to these pages for entertainment, rather than instruction. For those who wish to delve deeper into the subject, there will be ample reference in the introductory notes and in the appended list of recommended readings.

This is not primarily an art book, for I have dealt all too briefly with the artists and have given consideration only to the storytelling aspect of their work. I have adopted no special system or policy for selecting the pictures and have chosen those which deal with the most colorful and enticing myths or the most appealing of the gods or heroes. The pictures hang together merely on the thread of the story they illustrate. In style and period they are generally far apart. Although some of the world's greatest masterpieces are reproduced here, they play a secondary rôle, and must be considered as illustrations to the story which they enliven. But here surely is a distinguished roster of illustrators—Titian, Rubens, Correggio, Poussin and Turner, to name a few.

It will soon be obvious how vast and varied is the material, the pictorial as well as the literary. Despite the ravages of time, there are still preserved thousands of Greek terra-cotta vases bearing incisive drawings which depict the adventures of gods and heroes. There are countless statues and carvings, too, in the museums of many lands, which deal with this material. And the myths themselves are myriad and have been repeated and retold so often down through the years, that we hardly realize how much they have become a part of our everyday thinking and our everyday locutions. How many of us glibly use such expressions as "his Achilles heel" or "I fear the Greeks, even when they bear gifts" or refer to the "Labors of Hercules" or the "song of the Sirens" and remember the contexts out of which the phrases have been drawn?

I have chosen to ignore the more serious aspects of mythology. There is no attempt here to interpret the philosophy underlying a tale, or to point out its similarity to myths of other cultures, or to date its earliest occurrence in literature. We approach our subject like children wanting to believe in fairy tales and magic and the impossible. I have taken material from those sources deemed best for that purpose; from the pages of Ovid, Apuleius or Homer, the magnificent plays of Aeschylus, Sophocles and Euripides, and from many another writer and poet.

The book begins, then, with the Greek version of the Creation and its similarity to the Old Testament account is at once apparent. The battle of the gods and Titans finds its parallel in the aspirations of Lucifer and his cohorts. Eve's counterpart is Pandora, and Noah and his wife, like Deucalion and Pyrrha, are confronted with the problem of founding a new race, after a huge flood has wiped the earth clean of man and beast.

No goddess has been pictured more often than Venus. She was ever the symbol of supreme physical beauty. To Venus, then, is dedicated a chapter. We will hear her story, and see how she was imagined by many painters long since dead. We will find her pictured on the walls of Pompeii (which was buried by the eruption of Vesuvius in 79 A.D.), and in the bedchambers of lecherous kings of the eighteenth century.

Another chapter is devoted to the loves of Zeus. Here was a subject which caught the fancy of many painters. Zeus, or Jupiter, as he was also known, was a lusty god who pursued anything but a godly course. When from his Olympian heights he spied a seductive nymph or mortal, he took full advantage of all the magic at his disposal. In the form of a cloud, or a shower of gold, or a white bull, he descended from his godly abode to make love to Io or Danaë or Europa. His wife Hera was jealous and did her best to prevent these deceptions. These are the stories we will read, and the pictures we will see.

There will be tales of adventure, too. We will follow Jason and his Argonauts on their quest of the Golden Fleece. . . . We will suffer with Hercules when he performs his many Labors. To enjoy these verbal and pictorial re-creations of the old myths to the full, we must be ready to believe . . . or at least to dream! This is not stuff for the skeptic!

And then we will come to the Trojan War. The

stories, in their earliest form, are not for the squeam-
ish, for they are cruel and bloodthirsty, and by our
present-day standards, there are few good people, even
among the gods and heroes. But this is the material
out of which great playwrights fashioned some of
the most powerful tragedies which the world of literature has produced. Here only a few representative
stories and pictures have been selected to illustrate a
war which was waged for ten years. Perhaps these
will be sufficient to induce us to read further about
fair Helen, over whom Greeks and Trojans waged
such bloody battles. And surely, at some future time,
if we come upon other pictured episodes inspired by
Homer's mighty lines, we will find fuller understanding and experience greater excitement.

And at the end, we will deal with the adventures of
Ulysses, most crafty of the Greeks. We will follow
him in pictures and prose as he wanders for ten years
after the close of the Trojan War, to return finally to
his faithful wife. We will rejoice at his fierce vengeance when he slays the greedy suitors.

I hope, then, that the stories and pictures included
between the covers of this book will serve as spring-
boards for the imagination, and will help to rouse
from those regions where they dwell, the ghosts of
Hector and Helen, Prometheus and those others who
have given this work its meaning.

—HERMAN J. WECHSLER

1950

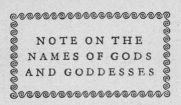

It will be apparent in the stories that follow that I have taken certain liberties with the names of the characters. The tales derive at times from Greek originals and at others from Roman sources. Most of the gods and goddesses have more than one name. Zeus is also known as Jove or Jupiter. Hera is commonly called Juno. Mercury and Hermes are one and the same.

There is, therefore, here provided a helpful guide to indicate the variants in the names of some of the characters.

Most painters, in giving titles to their pictures, have used the Roman and not the Greek names. And the most prolific writers after Homer, and the Greek dramatists, have written in Latin. Therefore, in the pages of this book, I have favored the Roman names, and if offense has been given to the spirits of those ancient Greeks who give this book its meaning, I hope to win forgiveness by making the proper and required sacrifices at some future date.

—H.J.W.

Some of the gods and goddesses mentioned in this book ... alternate names by which they were known.

GREEK	ROMAN
Zeus	Jupiter, also Jove
Hera	Juno, also Saturnia
Ares	Mars
Athena, or Athene	Minerva
Aphrodite	Venus, also Cytherea
Apollo, also Phoebus	Apollo, also Phoebus
Poseidon	Neptune
Hephaestus	Vulcan
Hades	Pluto
Artemis	Diana
Hermes	Mercury
Cronus	Saturn
Demeter	Ceres
Persephone	Proserpina, or Proserpine

GODS AND GODDESSES IN
Art and Legend

THE CREATION
THE GODS AND TITANS
PROMETHEUS AND PANDORA

FALL OF THE TITANS

*The defeated Titans were carried
down with the debris (pp. 2, 9)*

[DETAIL]

Rubens   *Musée de Ville, Brussels*

Plate 1

[DETAIL]

THE
CHILDHOOD OF
ZEUS

The child Zeus was nourished on the milk of a goat named Amalthea (pp. 3, 6)

[RIGHT]

HUNTING SCENE
OR
PRIMITIVE AGE OF MANKIND

Men fought not only the beasts of the forests but among themselves (pp. 3, 10)

Piero di Cosimo

Plate 2

Jordaens

Louvre, Paris

Plate 3

Metropolitan Museum of Art, New York

Signorelli

THE EDUCATION OF PAN

This was painted in an age when the artists looked to the pages of mythology for an excuse to depict the naked human form (p. 3)

Plate 4

Giovanni Bellini · Widener Collection, National Gallery of Art, Washington, D. C.

THE FEAST OF THE GODS

Bellini probably took his inspiration for this picture from the pages of Ovid. Here gods, satyrs and nymphs celebrate on the slopes of Mount Ida (p. 2)

Plate 5

Mantegna   *Louvre, Paris*

PARNASSUS
Mount of the Muses

The historic mountain is represented by Mantegna as a gay place where the muses dance to celebrate the love of Mars and Venus (p. 3)

Plate 6

Raphael · Vatican, Rome

PARNASSUS
Mount of the Muses
[DETAIL]
Raphael paints a more sober picture in which the enthralled muses listen to divine music (p. 3)

Plate 7

Titian   Prado, Madrid

PROMETHEUS

*Zeus ordered that a vulture should
each day devour the Titan's liver (pp. 3, 12)*

Plate 8

THE MOST commonly used source for the story of the Creation, the battle of Titans and gods, and the genealogy of the immortals and demigods, is the work of a Greek writer of the eighth or ninth century before Christ. Hesiod was a farmer who took upon himself the compilation of all material relating to these early beginnings. He lacked the epic genius of Homer, who used similar material and worked it into the drama of his exciting storytelling. Where Homer was a poet, Hesiod was a mere archivist. Unlike Ovid, who lived almost a thousand years later, he did not have the perspective, the temperament or the sense for the comic which would have enabled him to take the rich substance at his disposal and convert it into golden tales of love, magic and adventure.

In one of his books called *Works and Days,* Hesiod writes as a moralist, and attempts to tell mankind how to live a good and worthy life. In this work, there are many references to the gods and their behavior. But the main source-book for posterity is his *Theogony,* in which there are catalogued in rapid order a whole series of events, starting with the beginning of things. This does not afford exciting reading, for a tale which later storytellers embellished and expanded is here sometimes recorded in a single line. None the less, his was an inquiring mind, for he sought an explanation of the world's phenomena.

There is no skepticism in his heart, or so it seems, for he tells of the origin of things and the deeds of gods and monsters, just as he heard them. Perhaps his was an uncritical talent, but we are grateful to him for having left us this record which inspired so many later writers and artists.

The illustrations for this first chapter are not linked together in too coherent a fashion. The material here deals with the whole spectacle of the Creation, the war between gods and giants as well as the Flood, Prometheus and Pandora.

We have therefore selected a group of provocative paintings which fit the spirit, if not the content, of our introduction to mythology. Here, then, is a brief listing of the paintings:

There is a sketch by Rubens depicting "The Fall of the Titans," after their defeat by Zeus and the other gods (Plate 1).

Giovanni Bellini gives his version of a "Feast of the Gods" in which the faces and figures are those of fifteenth-century Italians, while the drapes and costumes represent his naïve notion of a pagan past (Plate 5).

Mantegna, a Renaissance master steeped in classical

2

lore, gives a poetic interpretation of Parnassus, Mount of the Muses, which may be compared with a painting by Raphael bearing the same title (Plates 6, 7).

Luca Signorelli paints a haunting picture of "The Education of Pan" (Plate 4).

We include one painting by Jordaens, who represents young Zeus, shortly after his birth, being nurtured by a nymph on the milk of the goat Amalthea (Plate 3).

Piero di Cosimo, a primitive Florentine, could have read Hesiod or Ovid or later works based on their writings, for his fanciful painting suggests one of the earliest "Ages of Man," as described in their pages (Plate 2).

The most gripping and heroic picture of all these is by Titian. He represents Prometheus bound to a rock in the Caucasus, with the vulture ready to peck at his liver (Plate 8).

This series of illustrations, then, will readily indicate how varied are the interpretations of our legendary material.

The Gods and Titans

Almost before the beginning of time itself and long before any of the gods and mortals whose stories will fill these pages were created, the world was in a state of Chaos. Water, air, and whirling clouds of gas mingled in a formless and changing mass. No growing thing or crawling beast existed in this Nothingness.

Then some Almighty Spirit brought order out of this confusion and the world as we know it began to take form. The waters of oceans, lakes and rivers found their places between the lonely stretches of flatland, gentle hills, and lofty mountains with their pinnacles rising to almost invisible heights. This lower region came to be known as Earth.

Then the gases cleared away and clean air stirred through the immeasurable empty spaces far beyond the highest peaks. Here the Moon and countless Stars found their home. Next came a more restless body called Sun and its journey across this upper realm of Heaven divided time into Day with its brightness and into Night with its frightening dark.

Now grass grew, and plants and flowers which gave color to the earth. Fish swam in the rivers and seas, and creatures of many shapes and sizes crawled through the damp forests or sunned themselves on river banks and stony ledges.

Next came the Titans, a mighty race of gigantic stature but well-proportioned and beautiful to behold. Of these there were twelve. There were monstrous creatures too, equal in size to the Titans but ugly and terrifying. Some were called Cyclopes and these had only one immense eye set in the middle of a vast forehead. And there were also giants with a hundred arms who could not be left to wander the earth, so brutal was their strength and so evil their ways. They

4

were therefore kept imprisoned deep down in the bowels of the earth in a lugubrious world called Tartarus.

The world was first inhabited by the Titans and the youngest and strongest of them was Cronus, who assumed leadership over all the rest. Cronus soon tired of ruling over a kingdom which boasted only beasts and speechless things and he summoned the Titan Prometheus and instructed him to make some more noble and exciting creature. This most thoughtful of the giants pondered at great length and at last molded out of soft clay a miniature of himself, counterfeit in all respects, except in beauty and in strength. Then he took up what he had wrought and set it before Cronus, who gazed with pleasure at the first man. Now Prometheus made more such, and Cronus gave them life and set them down on the earth where they managed to survive; for this was a Golden Age and there was as yet no hate and envy and men did not make war but lived in contentment off what the fruitful earth yielded. There were no seasons with their extremes of heat and cold, but only one eternal springtime.

Then, one day when his work was done, Cronus became aware of the tantalizing beauty of the Titan Rhea and he forthwith took her for his wife and queen. She bore him a child who brought him black fear in place of joy; he suddenly recalled a prophecy that if he were to have children, one among them would become more powerful than he and eventually dethrone him.

Now according to one record, Cronus had his child spirited away and imprisoned in a dismal place where no one might find it. But the ancient bard Hesiod has reported differently. Cronus in his abject fear swallowed his first child, thus furnishing for his offspring a strange and awful prison. And each baby as it was born was likewise swallowed by Cronus until Rhea lost all hope of ever rearing her young. When the sixth child was born, Rhea anticipated the visit of her husband and had the child carried away and hidden in a cave on the far-off island of Crete. Then she took a stone almost the size of the newborn infant, wrapped it in clothing and pretended to shelter it at her breast as one would do with a baby. Cronus was deceived and tore the "child" from her entreating arms and swallowed it as he had the others. Rhea pretended to weep and she wrung her hands and the Titan retired to his chamber secure in the knowledge that no son or daughter would ever challenge his power.

But Zeus, or Jupiter as another race came to call him, flourished in the care of a band of nymphs to whom he had been entrusted. They nourished him on the milk of a goat named Amalthea (Plate 3).

Zeus developed as no ordinary child, for at the age of one year he was tall and fully grown and already he was plotting against his father. It happened that Cronus visited the island of Crete and he was stunned to discover that here lived his son grown to manhood and already menacingly equal to him in physical prowess. He did not know that Zeus could rival him in cunning as well.

The son, then, pretended to greet his father with affection and respect and he announced a celebration to commemorate this first meeting. A cupbearer approached with a goblet of wine for King Cronus. Unsuspectingly he emptied it at one draught. But a drug had been mixed in the wine which so sickened the Titan that he began to vomit; there tumbled from his cavernous stomach all the five children along with the stone which had been substituted for Zeus.

While Cronus was still weak from his illness, Zeus called to his brothers and sisters to hasten away with him, knowing full well that once the Titan had recovered he would seek vengeance. Hurriedly they fled from Crete and established themselves on the heights of Mount Olympus, which was to be the home of the gods and goddesses—for so they called themselves from this time on.

When fully restored to his natural vigor, Cronus called all the Titans to an assembly and declared war on his rebellious children. Only three of the giants failed to comply with his request: old Iapetus and his sons, Prometheus and Epimetheus. Prometheus, who had the gift of foreknowledge, knew that in the coming war the gods and goddesses would ultimately be the victors. He therefore advised his father and brothers to remain neutral in the impending struggle.

But Cronus rallied his forces and the war was on.

The Titans who were loyal to him armed themselves with huge boulders and tall trees torn out of the forest. Then they began the ascent of Mount Olympus to oust the enemy from their fortified position. At this Zeus produced dark clouds to obscure the enemy's vision and flashed lightning in their eyes; and although they won positions far up the mountain several times, they were forced down again on each attempt. For ten years the war was waged and no side seemed to have a great advantage—except that the forces of Zeus still held their stronghold on the top of Olympus.

At last Cronus realized that the position of the gods and goddesses was apparently impregnable and he called a council of war and said to his men, "We are not making sufficient progress in this war. We must put ourselves in a position to cast down our ammunition upon the enemy and not be compelled, as heretofore, to climb so steep a hill. Let us build up a mountain even loftier than Olympus and from there we will easily hurl down our boulders and put them to rout." Then they went to work and tore huge pieces out of Mount Ossa and heaped these pieces one by one on Mount Pelion, knowing that when the one mountain was added to the other they would enjoy a position far above the home and fortress of their rivals.

Now Rhea, who feared for the welfare of her children, went to Zeus and told him of the plan. She also revealed to him that deep down in the earth were imprisoned the all-powerful Cyclopes along with the giants of a hundred arms. Even if they remained where they were these monsters could make the whole earth tremble when ordered to do so. The Cyclopes, on the other hand, knew the secret of forging thunderbolts and this was indeed a powerful weapon which the gods could well use.

Zeus now made the long journey to the underworld and offered to free these giants from their bonds if they would come to his aid. All readily agreed. The hundred-armed giants stationed below awaited their signal. As for the Cyclopes, Zeus led them up to Olympus, where they began immediately to forge their bolts.

Cronus meanwhile urged on his forces and soon the growing mountain was level with Olympus and threatened soon to overlook it. Now Zeus gave the signal. The Titans in the earth's center began to shake the world, so that the newly-made mountain shifted and started to collapse. From the Cyclopes' hands the gods seized the freshly wrought thunderbolts and these were hurled with devastating effect. Ossa and Pelion fell apart and carried down amid the debris all the Titans who were loyal to Cronus. With all hope gone, they now begged for mercy, knowing that victory had at last gone to the enemy (Plate 1).

But Zeus could find no mercy in his heart for the vanquished. He set apart the grim region of Tartarus as their prison; and after falling for nine days and nine nights, the giants reached this realm, to which they were condemned for eternity. Atlas, a son of Iapetus, was given a different punishment: he was condemned forever to bear the world on his shoulders. The aged Iapetus and his other sons, Prometheus and Epimetheus, were the only members of the vanquished race left free to roam the surface of the earth. Zeus was now supreme ruler of all the world.

Prometheus

After Zeus became king of heaven and earth, he began to make various experiments. The everlasting springtime he divided into seasons so that there was one season of extreme heat, one of extreme cold and two temperate seasons in between. This in turn led to other changes. Men were compelled to find or build shelters to protect themselves from the summer's heat or the winter's frost, the rains of spring and the cool autumnal winds. The change of seasons caused some plants to grow and some to die and man learned to cultivate the land and set aside portions of the crop for times when the land would be covered with snow.

Now, too, man began to hunt and he killed and devoured many beasts of the forest which hitherto had run free and unmolested. So a new kind of war was begun and often man was not the victor but the victim: frequently his cleaned bones would be found where some savage animal had left them. Some men were better clothed and better fed than others, and this caused quarrels and fighting. For the first time man was at war with man.

Prometheus, who had created man, looked down from Olympus and saw that something must be done for this race which he now identified with himself. He saw men who had once held their heads high, slink through the forests fearful for their lives. And the long hours of the night were the hardest to endure. So Prometheus went before his lord Zeus and begged that he be permitted to bring man fire to yield heat and light and protection.

But Zeus remembered only too well how quickly a race which has become proud and assured aspires to greater benefits and a nobler station. Had not he and his kindred wrested power from the Titans? So he refused fire to Prometheus and ordered him to ignore mankind and leave it to its plight, sorry though that might be.

But Prometheus could not be turned from his purpose. He found a reed well dried in the sun, and filled with pith. Then he hid himself one night close to the place where Phoebus Apollo began his blazing journey across the sky. As the god drove by, Prometheus held the reed against one of the fiery wheels and when it burst into flame he smothered it, and hid the glow so that none might see it. Then he descended to earth and brought fire to man and taught him its many uses. For the first time the earth-dwellers felt superior to the beasts. Prometheus begged that his secret be kept, knowing that when it was discovered he would pay dearly for his disobedience.

But one night Zeus saw a glow on earth as though

a firefly was flashing its light and he sent a messenger below to investigate. It was reported to him that man had now the use of this precious thing and Zeus guessed at once who had been the culprit. But he had no real proof.

Prometheus was now overconfident. Once again he sought to deceive his master. Zeus was furious at such arrogance and swore that the Titan who had once fought on his side but was now fallen from grace, would not go unpunished. He summoned two of the giants—Force and Violence they were named—who were even more powerful than the Flamegiver. He ordered them to carry Prometheus to the lonely peak of a mountain in the Caucasus. Hephaestus, later known as Vulcan, forged unbreakable fetters and with these Prometheus was bound to the rocks. Zeus further ordered that to assure an everlasting torture, a vulture should each day devour the Titan's liver (Plate 8). But each night the liver grew back. Zeus hoped that Prometheus would repent of his crime and he promised him freedom if he would reveal certain information to Zeus, for, as we recall, the Titan had foreknowledge of things to come. With unbelievable fortitude this great spirit refused to be threatened or bribed. He felt that what he had done for man was justified. Besides, had he not fought on the side of the gods in the hard war against his own people? And he knew too that one day in the dim future a hero would come to break his chains and give him freedom. Many, many centuries did Apollo drive his flaming chariot across the sky before this hero did come to free him from his torture. Though burdened with the performance of many labors, earthborn Hercules finally climbed the peak and unshackled Prometheus. And so was partially repaid mankind's debt to its greatest and most heroic champion.

Pandora

Although Zeus had avenged himself on the unruly Titan, there still remained the problem of making mankind pay a price for its crimes. And when he had considered this matter for some time, he finally knew that there was one sure way to torture man forever and ever. So he called Hephaestus to him and ordered him to make Woman.

Hephaestus was the most talented artificer among the gods. Once he so enraged his father that Zeus hurled him down from the heights of Olympus. He fell for three days and three nights before he struck the ground, and as a result of this fall he remained forever lame. He was the only child of Zeus and Hera who was not godlike in appearance, being ill-formed and unprepossessing. Not being endowed with the physical stamina of the other gods, he turned his attention to craftsmanship and the making of exquisite and useful objects. When he came to look for a wife he was given in marriage by a strange irony the most beautiful of all the goddesses—the ravishing Aphrodite, better known as Venus.

At any rate, Hephaestus fashioned Woman in the image of the goddesses—but smaller, more delicate, more finely made. When he brought this masterwork for Zeus to behold, the god of gods was pleased and called all the Olympians to see it. Then he gave the figure life and named it Pandora. He ordered that she be led down to earth and given as a bride to the Titan Epimetheus. Now Prometheus, suspecting trickery and evil, had warned his brother never to accept a gift from Zeus. But such was Pandora's beauty that the Titan received her willingly. The gods and goddesses had endowed the first woman with many gifts, unbelievable loveliness of face and figure, and had showered on her such gifts as fine raiment and jewels and flowers. But they also filled a chest with things evil: plagues, diseases and sorrow and despair. And Pandora was warned never to open the chest, but to leave it untouched in a corner of the dwelling which she shared with Epimetheus.

For a while Pandora was able to resist temptation but curiosity never stays far from where a woman is and one day the young bride raised the lid of the chest. Out flew all the evil things which had been imprisoned—all those things which henceforth would make mankind's lot miserable and hard to bear. Terrified, Pandora shut down the lid, but all the contents of the box had flown away to disperse themselves over the earth. One small thing remained, having been placed at the very bottom. This was Hope. And Hope alone was destined to alleviate for man the trials and sorrows which woman bequeathed him.

The Flood—Deucalion and Pyrrha

During the reign of Cronus there had been an Age of Gold, and this was followed by the Ages of Silver, of Bronze and of Iron. During this last period mankind became wicked. No longer was reverence shown for the gods; man was now avaricious and envious of his neighbor's wordly goods. He fought not only the beasts of the forests but his fellow man. Hate and Desire and Lust replaced the virtues of earlier times.

One day Zeus assumed the guise of a mortal and descended to earth to see for himself what were the ways of man. Such was the wickedness which he discovered that he decided to sweep all living things from the face of the earth. He feared to use thunderbolts, which might set not only the earth on fire but might all ascend to Olympus and destroy the palatial homes of the gods. He therefore caused huge and foreboding clouds to blot out the sun, and wild winds whirled down and blew across the face of the earth. Then the rains came, and with such fury did they pour down and so endless was the torrent that all was swept before it; hill after hill was covered and every living thing sought to climb higher and higher to be safe from the swirling waters. But even the mountains were soon covered; only one remained with its peak above the surface and this was Parnassus (later to be the home of the Muses), the highest mountain in the world. On its crest cringed the last remaining couple, Deucalion and Pyrrha, whom alone of all mankind Zeus found good and worthy of being saved.

At last the waters subsided and these two reverently built a temple to Zeus the Destroyer. They prayed and an oracle spoke to them and told them their destiny.

"Go," he said, "and take your Mother's bones and as you descend from Parnassus strew them behind you." At first the couple did not comprehend but soon Deucalion realized that Earth was mother of all things and that the stones and rocks were her bones.

So Deucalion and Pyrrha gathered up loose boulders on the mountain's peak and, in descending, threw them over their shoulders. When they fell on the earth these were transformed slowly into living things which soon assumed the shapes of men and women, a new race to people the earth. Thus began the Stone Age, and from this breed sprang the mortals whose stories will soon be told.

LOVES

OF

ZEUS

ZEUS
AND
IO

*Zeus in the
form of
a cloud
appeared
to Io
(pp. 18, 21)*

Correggio

*Vienna
Museum*

Plate 9

Titian

THE RAPE OF EUROPA

Before the startled girl could dismount,
they were moving rapidly over the water (pp. 18, 24)

Plate 10

Titian   Prado, Madrid

DANAË AND THE SHOWER OF GOLD

A shower of gold came
falling through the tower's opening (pp. 18, 26)

Plate 11

Titian   *Bridgewater House, London*

DIANA AND CALLISTO

Diana . . . expelled
Callisto from this favored company (pp. 18, 20)

Plate 12

VENUS—HER STORY

Botticelli

THE BIRTH OF VENUS

One morning
she floated ashore on a huge sea shell (pp. 28, 29)

Plate 13

Veronese   Metropolitan Museum of Art, New York

VENUS AND MARS

*The sun god Apollo was the first to be aware
of the secret meetings of Venus and Mars (pp. 28, 35)*

Plate 14

Titian

VENUS AND ADONIS

*The goddess . . . embraced Adonis and in
parting warned him, "For my sake be content to hunt
the timid and less fierce creatures of the woods"* (pp. 28, 34)

Plate 15

Boucher   *Louvre, Paris*

VENUS AND VULCAN

*Venus was given in marriage
to the least handsome of the gods (p. 28)*

Plate 16

Raoux   *Louvre, Paris*

PYGMALION, GALATEA AND VENUS

The goddess of love
granted Pygmalion his wish (pp. 28, 37)

Plate 17

Boucher

VENUS AND CUPID

*The goddess is here represented
in one of her quieter moments. The
present title is* Venus Consoling Love
(p. 28)

Plate 18

TRAGIC TALES

Poussin   Louvre, Paris

ECHO AND NARCISSUS

He could not bring himself to leave the water's edge
(pp. 39, 48)

Plate 19

Tiepolo

Louvre, Paris

DAPHNE AND APOLLO

"If you would help me," she cried,
"transform this beauty which is my undoing"
(pp. 39, 44)

Plate 20

Pollaiuolo National Gallery, London

DAPHNE AND APOLLO

In a moment her arms became graceful branches
(pp. 39, 44)

Plate 21

Claude Lorrain   National Gallery, London

NARCISSUS AND ECHO

Plate 22   [DETAIL]

Her love did not lessen and she wasted
away with grief and complaint
(pp. 40, 47)

Poussin   *Louvre, Paris*

ORPHEUS AND EURYDICE

Eurydice, in walking through the deep grass, was bitten on the foot by a poisonous snake (pp. 30, 41)

[DETAIL]   Plate 23

DEATH OF PROCRIS

So Procris died,
pierced by her lover's spear
through a tragic misunderstanding
(pp. 40, 46)

Piero di Cosimo
National Gallery, London

Plate 24

CHAPTER II

THE LOVES
OF ZEUS

I N GREEK MYTHOLOGY, the greatest of the gods was almighty Zeus. We have already learned of how he
came into power after conquering the fierce Titans.
His character is not too clearly defined in the many
stories in which he plays a rôle, and his behavior
would hardly entitle him to the awesome title of
"greatest of the gods" by any modern standards of
morality. He is often petty, selfish and jealous. When
called upon to make an important decision, he is
evasive, and passes this responsibility on to others.
At times, however, he reveals a nobler aspect, and
stands on the side of Truth and Justice. He intrudes
repeatedly in the affairs of other gods, and takes sides
in the battles of heroes.

But his appearance in the works of art from earliest
times comes mostly in the rôle of lover. This aspect
of his personality seems to have caught the fancy of
many painters. They were intrigued by the various
devices he used to deceive his wife, Hera.

To illustrate the stories in this section I have selected

representative paintings by the Venetian master, Titian, and the North Italian painter, Correggio.

Titian was a man of sound learning and like the artists, scholars, and poets of his time he turned to antiquity for inspiration and guidance. It was inevitable that the rich and varied subject matter of Greek fable should appeal to the temperament of such a man. He was no slave to the classical texts which he knew well and with this material took many liberties. The original story might have Danaë imprisoned in a house of bronze with no opening except to the sky. Titian none the less will place her on a divan in a setting rich with Renaissance drapes and hangings. Here she reclines like a courtesan of pagan Venice against the dramatic background of sky and distant landscapes. These Italians are not mere copyists or imitators. Antiquity supplied them with luxurious material and out of its substance they fashioned their own poetic statements (Plates 10, 11, 12).

Vasari describes the Lombard painter, Antonio da Correggio, as a man of timid disposition who never enjoyed the opportunity to travel to Rome and see antique statues or other works of art. However, in describing his painting of a nude Venus, Vasari writes that so entrancing "was her loveliness that it is hard to regard her delicateness and whiteness without emotion." Correggio made the characters of mythology fit his own concept of the ideal human form (Plate 9).

Zeus and the Nymph Callisto

Callisto was a nymph of rare beauty who followed Diana the Huntress as she and her maidens wandered the Arcadian woodlands. She was favored by Diana for her fidelity and her skill in the chase. One day she entered a deep forest and lay down to rest. Zeus caught sight of her as she slept, unprotected and enticing. "Here is a splendid opportunity to deceive my consort," he said. "And if I should be caught, it will be well worth the price in taunts and nagging!" Thereupon he transformed himself into the shape and guise of Diana herself, and awakened the slumbering girl. Callisto arose refreshed from her rest and greeted the false goddess with these words, "Welcome, my leader, nobler than Zeus himself. This I say, even though he might overhear my words." The great god, who was not without a sense of humor, was amused to find himself thus prized. Whereupon he kissed the nymph, and not too chastely. His ardor increased, and soon the poor huntress was fighting with all her girlish might. Hera might not have been so vindictive if she had witnessed this futile struggle. Having had his way, Zeus returned to his Olympian home, and unhappy Callisto wandered the woodland alone and ashamed. She dared not tell Diana of her misfortune.

One summer day, months later, the Divine Huntress and her followers left the chase to cool their bodies in a pleasant stream. All disrobed at once.

But blushing Callisto made excuses and delayed. Her companions forced her to undress, but immediately sought to hide her plight. However, Diana became aware at once of what had happened, and in her anger she expelled Callisto from her favored company (Plate 12).

Now it seems that Hera had long since known of her husband's escapade, but she waited until now to have her revenge. When the nymph gave birth to a son, Arcas by name, Hera's frenzy knew no limits. She seized the poor girl by the hair, and threw her face forward to the ground. And when Callisto stretched out her arms in supplication, they were no longer human arms, but black with shaggy fur. She strove to speak, but uttered only a terrifying growl. Hera had transformed her into a bear. Her feelings, however, were still human. In misery she roamed the very woodlands where once she had proudly held sway.

The years passed and her son Arcas grew to young manhood. Hunting in the Arcadian woods one day, he came upon his mother thus transformed. He was puzzled by the manner in which the frightened animal stared at him, but was none the less about to pierce her breast with his spear.

Finally contrite, Zeus decided to intervene. Sending a whirlwind to catch up mother and son, he set them down among the stars in the heavens. She, whom Hera had driven out of human form, was now a goddess! There was little that Hera could do. Only this small satisfaction was hers: she asked of the God of the Sea that the Great and Little Bear, unlike the other stars, should never be permitted to descend into the ocean. Her wish was granted. And if you observe the heavens closely, you will find that these constellations never dip below the horizon.

The Story of Io

Io was a maiden of surpassing beauty. One day Zeus saw her coming from the stream of her father, Inachus, a river god. "Here is a maid worthy of my love," he said to himself. "If you are fearful of wild beasts," he told her, "go unafraid under my protection. For I am not one of those lesser gods!" Perhaps Io had heard tales about her would-be champion, for she immediately took to flight. Whereupon Zeus, to vary his playful habit, caused a dark cloud to descend upon the sunny landscape (Plate 9). Concealed, or so he thought, by this covering, he overtook the frightened maid, and had his will of her.

Now Hera chanced to look down on the sunny vales of Argos. She was puzzled when she noted that one area alone was dark with nightshades. And Zeus was away from home! She quickly descended to earth, and ordered the clouds to disperse.

Zeus must have had warning, for before the mists had cleared away, Io, the daughter of Inachus, had been transformed by him into a heifer of extravagant

21

beauty. Hera understood. But none the less, she pretended ignorance, and asked from what herd this wonderful creature had strayed. Zeus was not his usual resourceful self, and said simply that she had risen suddenly out of the ground. Hera then demanded the heifer as a gift, and the faithless lover consented, rather than make confession.

Mute and helpless, Io listened to her betrayal. Hera, fearful of some further treachery by her spouse, gave the heifer into the keeping of Argus, he of a hundred eyes. Only two eyes were closed at a time, and the others watched and guarded Io. By day she grazed, but at night she was tethered with a halter round her tender neck.

One day she wandered down to the stream of her father, Inachus, but neither he nor her sisters recognized her. Io finally traced out her story in the dust, forming the letters with her hoofs. Her father read the message and wept. Argus soon separated them, and drove unhappy Io to more distant pastures.

By this time, Zeus could not bear sad Io's sufferings, and he sent Mercury to slay Argus and release the heifer from captivity. Mercury approached Argus disguised as a shepherd, and lulled the monster to sleep with sweet melodies from his reed pipe. Then Mercury uncovered his sword, and cut through the sleeper's neck. The head rolled down the mountainside, but Hera took the hundred eyes and set them in the tail of the peacock, where we may still find them.

Io was not yet completely free. Hera sent a gadfly

to plague her, and she wandered far and wide in her plight. Finally, she came to the river Nile, and at the water's edge, she prayed once more to Zeus. He heard her plaint, and begged Hera to put aside her vengeance. The goddess consented at last, and Io's tortures were at an end.

On the banks of the ancient river, she once again took on her former shape, with all its early grace and beauty.

The Rape of Europa

Europa was the daughter of the King of Sidon, and she was destined to go with the almighty Zeus on a long and strange journey. She suffered not at all at the hands of the great god, and aside from her initial fright, hers was a happy adventure.

On a pleasant morning in early spring, the leader of the gods was idly contemplating the earth below him. This is what he saw:

Europa had spent a sleepless night, with troubling dreams to disturb her slumber. So she arose just after dawn and called to her companions to join her at a favored spot down near the ocean's verge. Here they would sport and dance and finally bathe in cool waters. They plucked hyacinths and narcissus and violets and the blossoms of the wild rose. All the girls were lovely, but fair Europa was lovelier still, and Zeus, of course, was quick to appraise her startling beauty. Now in this

23

adventure, at least, all the blame was not with lusty Zeus. Hera was away from home, but the god seemed content to stay on Olympus, satisfying himself with mere contemplation of the scenes below. But Venus, or the ever playful Cupid, aimed an arrow at his heart, just as he was following the graceful movements of fair Europa. There was nothing now for the love-sick god to do but start off on another adventure.

Quickly he changed himself into a bull, but such a one as had never been seen in heaven or on earth. His color was pure white, like the snow before it has been melted by the warm winds of the south. He was perfectly formed, and he seemed tame and friendly. Even the timid girls were unafraid, and approached this beautiful creature. They offered him flowers to taste, and he kissed their outstretched hands.

Europa, more daring than the rest, sat upon his back, whereupon he slowly moved down to the water's edge. Suddenly his movements quickened, and before the startled girl could dismount, they were moving rapidly over the water (Plate 10).

Europa knew now that this was no ordinary bull, and she begged to be set down among her companions on the rapidly disappearing shore. But Zeus told her to have no fear. He quieted her trembling and in-formed her that their destination was the island of Crete, a place he knew well, for he had once hidden there from the Titan, Cronus. There, he said, they might live quietly and in peace, as lovers should.

It all happened as Zeus promised. Upon arrival,

Europa was dressed by the Seasons for her marriage ceremony. For a long time she lived a serenely happy life, and here she bore Zeus several famous sons.

Danaë and the Shower of Gold

Acrisius, the King of Argos, had a daughter whose beauty was so great that all men marveled to behold it. Her name was Danaë.

But the King was a bitter man, for he had hoped for a son to carry on his noble line. One day he sent a messenger to the city of Delphi, where dwelt a famous oracle, and of him he asked if he was destined to have a son.

The oracle made answer that Danaë, his daughter, would bear a male child, and that this child would inherit the kingdom of Acrisius. But the oracle also added an ominous note to his prophecy: this same child would be the cause of the king's death.

Acrisius was terrified. He was reluctant to have Danaë killed, and bethought himself of a plan to keep her hidden from the eyes of man.

So he ordered wrought a house of bronze, with no windows and only a single door, to which he kept the key. This house, or tower, was sunk into the ground, and light and air came only through the top. Danaë might never again see fields and running streams and grazing cattle, but only the sky above. Here she remained alone, with only an old nurse to serve her.

But Acrisius had not counted on Zeus, from whom

nothing might be hid—especially a beautiful girl. One day, as she lay bored and desolate in her prison home, a shower of gold came falling through the tower's opening (Plate 11). This was no ordinary gold, however, but Zeus himself. When he left Danaë's side, he did so as a glittering stream, which rose gracefully to the skies.

And then one day a lusty son was born to Danaë. This could not be hid from the King. When he saw the child, and remembered the words of the oracle, he was sorely frightened. Perhaps he suspected almighty Zeus, for he dared not slay this child. He therefore ordered a huge chest to be made and in it he placed Danaë and the newborn infant. Down to the angry sea the chest was taken and set afloat.

But Acrisius had not reckoned with the inexorable decisions of Fate. The sea became calm, and the breezes soft and warm. The chest drifted slowly across the untroubled waters and came to rest finally on a foreign shore, in a country called Seriphus.

Dictys, a fisherman, and a brother of the king of this land, found Danaë and her son.

He was a good man, and childless, and he took Danaë and the boy to live with him in his humble hut at the sea's edge. Here they were treated with kindness by Dictys, as son and daughter.

The child flourished and grew to young manhood, and was of exceeding beauty, grace and strength.

Perseus was the name given to him, and we shall meet him again in the pages of this book.

CHAPTER III

VENUS—
HER STORY

CERTAINLY NO OTHER goddess in the Olympian hier-
archy is so often mentioned in our daily speech
as Venus, the personification of earthly love and
earthy beauty. From the earliest times she represented
to man the utmost in physical perfection, and she was,
as we shall see, the forerunner of all "beauty contest"
winners.

It was inevitable, therefore, that artists, painters
and sculptors alike, should represent her over and over
again. In earlier centuries she was usually depicted as
playing some rôle out of legend or myth. We see her
competing for the prize offered by Paris, or playing
with her son, Cupid, or consorting with the other
gods. Among the artists few made her a languorously
graceful maiden, as did Botticelli, the Florentine who
was a poet and dreamer among painters.

The later painters of the Renaissance, especially the
Venetians, represented her generally as an extrava-
gantly exotic female, languishing in a rich setting,
where she seems usually to be awaiting a courtly lover.
There is no longer a pretense of relating her to the

character who appears in the pages of Homer or the other classical authors, and now the term "Venus" is practically no more than a synonym for a beautiful woman. In the eighteenth century, many a king's mistress posed nude for the favorite court painter, and although all France must have recognized her features, the official title given the painting was something like "Venus Reclining on a Divan" or "Venus at her Mirror."

The pictures included in this volume begin with Botticelli's "Birth of Venus" (Plate 13).

The painting by Titian is inspired by her episode with Adonis. She is shown trying to dissuade him from leaving her side to go off to the hunt (Plate 15).

There is a painting by Veronese, in which the goddess appears with Mars who is represented as a handsome and exceedingly virile soldier worthy of her love (Plate 14).

In the painting by Raoux, she plays a lesser role, and is shown hovering overhead with her son, Cupid, at the moment when Galatea comes to life to surprise her lover, Pygmalion (Plate 17).

There are, lastly, two eighteenth century paintings by Boucher. In the one, she is shown with her husband, Vulcan; in the other, with her son, Cupid. In the art of Boucher, Venus has come down from the skies, and into the bedchamber (Plates 16, 18).

Venus, Goddess of Love

Some pages from her life story, including her love for Adonis ... The Evil She Brought Atalanta and Hippomenes ... An Episode with Mars ... The Good She Brought to Pygmalion and Galatea.

Concerning the childhood of Aphrodite, or Venus, as she is better known, we know very little, for one day she rose out of the sea full-grown and in possession of all that beauty of form and countenance which was to make her the darling of the gods—the male gods that is, for among the women she found many enemies and few friends. In the heavenly abode of Olympus she caused havoc enough among the immortals, but when she came down to earth to display her charms before Paris, son of Priam, she was indirectly the cause of a war which lasted for ten years.

Birth of Venus

There is a story told of the birth of the goddess which makes her the daughter of great Zeus and Dione,—but to this we give little credence. There are more authoritative sources which in great detail describe how one morning she floated ashore on a huge sea shell, having been formed deep at sea out of the sea's own foam (Plate 13). Her very name proves this to be true, for Aphrodite is the Greek word

29

for "foam-risen." Gentle zephyrs rippled the calm waters and slowly she drifted to shore, there to be received by the Hours, gentle maidens who dressed her nakedness in the raiment of the immortals and led her before the gods of Olympus. This birth of Venus took place in the sea near Cythera, but when she came ashore, it was on the island of Cyprus, and for this reason you will discover in the many stories about her that sometimes she is called Cytherea and sometimes the Cyprian.

When she was brought before the Olympians, all the gods desired her, but Zeus gave her to Vulcan.

It is now time to tell of the son of Venus, Cupid or Eros, as he was variously called. The bow and quiver of arrows which his mother gave him he used sometimes to good and sometimes to evil effect. Some of the arrows had tips of gold, and these, when they pierced a human breast, aroused sentiments of love and desire. There were other arrows which aroused the reverse feeling of hate and antipathy. One day, when Venus was playing with her prank-loving son, she accidentally pricked her own breast with one of the gold-tipped arrows. She was as unaware of this, so slight was the wound, as of the fact that at that very moment she had been gazing down on earth watching young Adonis returning from the hunt. She was of course now hopelessly in love with him. And being in love with an earth-dweller, she came down from her Olympian palace, ignored her favored haunts in Cythera and

Paphos and followed the young hunter wherever he wandered. She forgot her salves and paints and sweet-smelling perfumes and no longer spent endless hours before the mirror making her toilet. Instead, she garbed herself in the manner of the divine Huntress, Diana, and joined Adonis in the chase. When the moment came for rest and refreshment, she fed him mostly with kisses, and if at times he seemed satiated, she enlivened the interludes with stories about herself, thus pleasantly filling in the intervals until his ardor was again aroused. One day, as they lay in the shade of a tall poplar, she repeated the tale of

Atalanta and Hippomenes

Atalanta was a maid who was famed far and wide for her bewitching beauty, as well as for her fleetness of foot. Once, when she consulted an oracle, she was warned never to take a husband, for only misfortune could be her lot. And although she had a healthy maiden's desire for a lover and companion, she invented many excuses to dissuade the anxious suitors. When they continued to besiege her, she announced that only he who could outrun her in a footrace would win her as a bride. The prize, therefore, was a beautiful virgin, but the penalty for being beaten in the contest was death!

One day, young Hippomenes was a spectator at such a trial and at first he thought it absurd that any man should wager such a heavy stake for the winning of a mere woman. Then he had his first sight of Atalanta. She was ready and eager at her mark and as she had disrobed for the race, Hippomenes had an opportunity to appraise the rare beauty for which so many men in the prime of youth were risking their lives. He, too, was now enamored of her.

The first contest was over and Atalanta was still panting from her efforts, when the cries of the unfortunate victim were heard. Now Hippomenes approached the girl and offered to test his fleetness against hers. When she saw that his beauty matched her own, she tried to dissuade him; for she loved him on the instant of beholding.

Meanwhile Hippomenes had raised up his voice in prayer to Venus and a gentle breeze carried the words to Olympus. Hurriedly she came to his aid and on her journey across Cyprus she plucked three apples of shining gold from a wonderful tree which grew there.

Now the trumpets sounded for the race to begin. Venus, invisible to all except the daring youth, appeared to him and gave him the apples, instructing him meanwhile in their use. Once again the signal sounded and the race was on. Hippomenes was swiftly off his mark, but he held the lead for only a moment. Reluctantly the fleet Atalanta passed him on the first stretch of the race, gazing as she flew by at his handsome countenance, bitter at the thought of what victory would mean. Hippomenes threw the first apple so that it rolled well ahead of the flying girl, and somewhat off the course. Eager to possess this ball of gold, she shortened her strides and stopped for an instant to pick it up. Meanwhile, her rival burst ahead as the spectators roared their approval, for they too were saddened by the spectacle of so many boys in the first flush of youth going down to the dark corridors of Hades.

Now in possession of her lovely bauble, Atalanta again overtook her rival. As before, he tossed an apple so that it slowed the girl in her flight when she stooped to pick it up. Once again, the tiring lad was in the lead. The goal now was in sight and Atalanta was running neck and neck with Hippomenes, when he threw the last of the apples. She hesitated for only an instant, sensing the risk she took. The gleaming ball lay well off to the side of the course, but, thinking she could still win the race, she swerved from the track to scoop it up. By now, the lad was again out in front and she hastened to overtake him. But Venus increased the weight of the apples of gold which she was loath to throw away and this encumbrance was just sufficient to cause her to lag a breath behind as the finish line was crossed. The spectators shouted their approval and Hippomenes led off his prize.

Venus interrupted her story; then, between kisses she continued, "You would think, O beloved Adonis, that for such services this fortunate couple would burn incense at my altar. But not one word of thanks was spoken and no sacrifice was made! I decided then to be avenged for this slight. As they were walking

33

through the woods and passed close by an ancient temple sacred to the gods, I aroused in Hippomenes such a lust that there, where the priests usually set up their tripods, he defiled the sanctuary with his love-making! Punishment came from above with lightning speed. On the necks of the pair manes began to grow. The fingers became claws, their arms changed to fur-covered legs. Bushy tails swept the ground, and growls were uttered in place of human speech. Lion and lion-ess now looked upon one another!"

The goddess, having finished her story, embraced Adonis in a long farewell and in parting, warned him, "For my sake, be content to hunt the timid and less fierce creatures of the woods, and turn your back in flight if lion or tigress or wild boar approach you!" (Plate 15).

Then, mounting her chariot, she took to the air, casting many a backward glance at her lover. No sooner was she gone than Adonis roused himself for the hunt, and ignoring her admonition, he followed the tracks of a wild boar. As soon as his hounds had cornered the beast, he let fly his spear, but succeeded only in wounding the animal. The enraged beast turned upon him, and in an instant sunk its long tusk deep into his body. The groans of the dying lad reached Venus as she sped heavenward. Quickly she returned to earth to find a lifeless form which could respond no more to her warm kisses and hard em-brace. She tore her garments and beat her breast, to no avail.

Only this was she able to do to commemorate her grief: she sprinkled the fresh blood on the soil and within an hour, where it had soaked into the ground, a bright red flower grew. This came to be called the anemone, or wind-flower, for its life is short and almost as soon as it reaches full growth, the wind comes to scatter its bloom over the earth.

Venus and Mars

One of the most oft-told stories in heaven (for gods and goddesses enjoy gossip as much as do mortals) was that of how Vulcan learned that his wife was deceiving him, and how he had his revenge. Apollo was the first to be aware of the secret meetings of Venus and Mars (Plate 14). This he reported to Vulcan one day when he was at work on some commission. After he had recovered from the shock, the lame god proceeded to fabricate a net of bronze with links of such incredible delicacy and fineness that the mesh was invisible to the naked eye. It had, indeed, all the softness and suppleness of a spider's web. This he spread over his own marriage couch, then hid himself nearby. When Venus and her paramour had stretched themselves upon it, he drew it fast and held them thus imprisoned in close and shameful embrace. Then he threw wide the doors to the bedchamber and all the gods and goddesses were called in to see the spectacle. One of the gods, however, was overheard to say that this was the kind of crime in which he would willingly be caught. All laughed at this sprightly remark, and the Olympians regaled themselves at many a banquet with the retelling of this story.

Pygmalion and Galatea

Pygmalion was a young artist of Cyprus who had no use for womankind. He lived the life of a celibate and spent his time in making figures of great beauty out of stone, ivory and precious metals. One day, out of whitest ivory, he carved the statue of a maiden with face and form of such divine proportions that he fell in love with his own handicraft. He named this lifeless thing Galatea. Often he ran his hands over the ivory maid, half expecting the flesh to yield to his touch. He kissed the lips again and again, but found them cold and unresponsive. He spoke words of love which remained unanswered. Maddened with unassuaged passion, he brought trinkets and gifts of many kinds and laid them at the feet of the statue. He secured gowns of rarest fabric and draped them on the naked form and added necklaces and rings and bracelets, all the adornments so prized by women. At night he gently placed the figure on a bed in his chamber and spread coverlets over it as though to keep it warm.

Then came the feast day of Venus and all Cyprus gathered for the celebration. Sacrifices were made to the goddess of love, and countless prayers were spoken.

Pygmalion came with the rest and having laid his offering on the altar, he breathed, "O Goddess, if you are good to lovers as they tell, and powerful to perform miracles, give me for wife my ivory maid!" Shamefaced, he uttered these words and disconsolately returned to his home.

But Venus had heard his plea. When Pygmalion entered his chamber, he leaned over as usual to kiss the statue. As he gathered the form to him, it seemed warm to the touch and yielded where his fingers strayed. His kisses were not coolly received now, for the lips which eagerly met his were the lips of a young girl pulsating with life and desire. As her eyes slowly opened, Galatea saw the light and beauty of the universe and her lover for the first time (Plate 17).

Venus herself came to their wedding and rejoiced in their happiness.

These, then, are some of the stories about Venus. They represent only a few episodes in her colorful career. There are, besides, many stories of her affairs with other gods and mortals, but some of these I judge untrue; for, being a beautiful woman, she was the victim of much false and calumnious gossip.

THE MATERIAL for these four short stories of tragic love I have taken principally from the writings of Ovid, a Roman poet of the time of Augustus. To the telling of these tales, he brought a superb gift for sensuous imagery, and his *Metamorphoses,* a compendium of almost all the stories of classical mythology, was the favored sourcebook of many artists, who translated his exotic descriptions into visual representations. Singlehanded, he produced the most complete handbook of Greek mythology; not only later mythographers, but most of the English poets, are greatly in his debt.

Ovid was born in 43 B.C., into a "good family." He revealed an early love for poetry and not, as his parents had hoped, for the law or public life. He published some passionate lyric verses while still a young man, and these were well-known and popular in his town. In the year 8 A.D., he was banished from his homeland by imperial decree. The Emperor Augustus gave as the reason, the immorality of his love poems.

For paintings to illustrate the following tales, there

are works of masters ranging from the fifteenth to the eighteenth centuries. In two instances, we have the opportunity to compare highly diverse treatments of the same theme.

Antonio Pollaiuolo, a fifteenth century Florentine, represents Apollo and Daphne silhouetted against a charming contemporary Italian landscape. The scenery, in all its detail, is handled with care and affection, for this love of the physical universe is a new note in Italian painting (Plate 21).

Giovanni Battista Tiepolo, a painter of eighteenth-century Venice, brings the magic of a brilliant and lush palette to the telling of the same story. Daphne is shown at the moment of transformation. Every movement of the body is well observed and perfectly rendered. The very leaves which sprout from her fingertips are true to nature (Plate 20).

Poussin, a seventeenth century French painter, spent most of his time in Italy and became the most Italianate of French masters. His love of things classical was profound. In a landscape of idyllic beauty, we find Narcissus dying of self-love, while a wraithlike Echo mourns nearby (Plate 19).

In the myth of Orpheus and Eurydice, the setting is a contemporary Roman landscape. Orpheus plays his lyre to an admiring audience, all unheeding of Eurydice's plight, for she has just been bitten by a poisonous snake, and is doomed to die (Plate 23).

Claude Lorrain, another French master of the seventeenth century, was essentially a painter of nature.

The landscape is an enormous "backdrop" against which the drama of the myth becomes a petty incident. And poor Echo wastes away in futile yearning for her beloved Narcissus (Plate 22).

Although the story of Cephalus and Procris has never been widely known, several artists have used it for subject matter. In his version of the story Piero di Cosimo paints dead Procris, mourned by a faithful dog and a Satyr (Plate 24).

Orpheus and Eurydice

Orpheus was born of the love of one of the Muses, Calliope, and a young prince of Thrace. Some say his father was the sun-god, Apollo. The gift of making enchanting music he had from his mother, and it is told that all who listened were held spellbound by his playing. Not only gods and mortals, but the very rocks and streams were affected by the dulcet tones of his lyre.

Perhaps it was his music that first attracted the maiden Eurydice; perhaps it was the beauty of his person. They were united and Hymen, god of marriage, himself came for the ceremony. But his serious mien betokened no good fortune for the young couple. The torch which Hymen carried sputtered and smoked and would not catch fire. All knew that this was an ill omen. Immediately after the wedding, Eurydice, in walking through the deep grass, was bitten on the foot by a poisonous snake, and fell dead at the feet of her lover (Plate 23).

Orpheus mourned his bride in the upper world and finally decided to go down among the shades in their Stygian realm. He came before Persephone and Hades, the rulers of the dead. Then he took out his lyre, plucked its strings and began to sing to its plaintive melody. He told them in song that he dared descend to the underworld only to see his wife, whose love he had enjoyed for so brief a span. He begged that she be released to live out the years that were her lot, above in the world of light and flowers.

Orpheus could not be denied. Eurydice was summoned, and when she appeared she was still limping from her fresh wound. And it was ordained that she might return with her lover to the world above. But there was one condition: Orpheus must not turn his eyes backward in his journey from the nether world; if he did, the gift of a new life for his bride was all in vain.

Slowly the pair began their journey through the lugubrious realm of the dead. They had almost reached the outer world, with its sunny fields and carpet of flowers. Orpheus led the way and Eurydice walked behind him slowly, for her foot was not yet mended. And then the anxious lover turned his gaze backwards and in that instant she was gone, slipped back into the darkness of Dis. Dying a second time, fair Eurydice made no complaint, for she knew that this misfortune came of the great love her husband bore her. She called out one last farewell, and was gone forever.

Orpheus, stunned and broken-hearted, begged again to cross the Styx, but was driven back. For seven days he sat on the dark river's edge. He did not eat, but only bemoaned his loss. Maidens and nymphs loved and sought him, but all were repulsed. Disconsolately he wandered the Thracian hills and countryside. One day, a band of Maenads encountered the sad music maker and slew him, tearing his very limbs apart in their fury. These they threw into the swift stream of the river Hebrus. It is recorded that Muses on the island of Lesbos found the unchanged remains of his mortal body and buried them with all due honor. But Orpheus had long since crossed the river Styx for the second time, where he was reunited forever with his beloved Eurydice.

Daphne and Apollo

Daphne was the daughter of the river god Peneus. The tragedy which befell her was caused by a dispute between Apollo and young Cupid. One day, the sun god watched the youthful archer, son of Venus, adjusting his bow. He remarked sarcastically, "What are you, a mere child, doing with a man's weapon? The bow and arrow are meant for such as I, a mature man and a hunter. With it I slay worthy foes and wild and dangerous beasts. Why do you dare to compete with me, with that toy that slays nought, but produces only love-pains with its flimsy darts?"

"O haughty Apollo," the son of Venus replied angrily, "great huntsman though you be, your arrows may find whatever mark they choose, but your noble breast will now be my target!"

Cupid stretched his bow and let fly an arrow of lead at young and beautiful Daphne. A dart of gold a moment later pierced Apollo's noble breast and he was at once sick with love for the daughter of Peneus.

Thus did the god love and the young girl hate. She fled all suitors, roaming the forests and fleeing the approach of all men, however handsome their mien. Her father would chide her and say, "Daughter, it is time you were wed. You should have a husband and I a grandson." But Daphne would blush as she clung to her father's neck, and pray that like Diana, she might ever remain a virgin. With sadness in his heart, her father granted this unnatural request. And as Apollo watched the graceful girl run through the forest, his love burned hot to the very marrow. He called to the nymph and begged her to stay in her flight. "I am no enemy," he called, "but a lover who seeks to woo you tenderly. I am no unkempt shepherd who pursues you, but the son of Jove himself. And I am sick with love of you."

As he ran, he continued his plea, but the girl paid no heed. She was indeed beautiful in her flight. Her garments, all aflutter, bared her graceful limbs, and her hair streamed behind in long locks.

The chase was to end soon. Apollo gained on the tiring girl. Soon his breath was hot on her neck. Knowing that she was about to be overtaken, she called to her father to keep his promise. "If you would help me," she cried, "transform this beauty which is my undoing!" (Plate 20)

Her prayer was hardly done when a numbness seized her limbs and thin bark began to replace her glowing skin. In a moment her hair was changed to leaves, her arms became graceful branches, her feet were rooted to the earth (Plate 21). Even now Apollo loved her, but his embrace found only a laurel tree which still quivered in fear and underneath the bark, a heart beat fitfully.

Cephalus and Procris

Cephalus and Procris were a happily married couple, but their bliss was destined to be short-lived. Soon after the young pair were wedded, Aurora, goddess of the dawn, chanced to see young Cephalus and immediately fell in love with him. Against the lad's will, she carried him off to her abode on the top of Mount Hymettus. The unhappy boy told Aurora repeatedly that he was incapable of loving anyone but Procris. He thought only of his young bride and her name was ever in his heart and on his lips. The goddess was angered at this and in her fury finally exclaimed, "Keep your Procris and go back to her! But you will repent one day of ever having loved her!"

This prophecy troubled Cephalus and was the cause of mistrust and misunderstanding. But for the time being all was righted and the pair again lived very happily. Procris made her young husband two wonderful gifts—a hound for the chase that none other could outrun and a javelin that, when thrown, always found its mark. Now it was the custom of Cephalus to hunt in the woods and when he was tired, to seek the quiet of some sequestered spot. Lying on his back, he would welcome the cool winds which blew gently on his heated body. He would call out aloud, "Gentle Aura [this was the name of a breeze], come and relieve this heat in me! Let me feel your perfumed breath on my face!" He was overheard by some gossip who returned to Procris to tell of her husband's deception.

So Procris now believed that the young hunter was enamored of a nymph called Aura. At times she doubted the tale, for Cephalus was as kind and affectionate as ever. But at other times, the pangs of jealousy caused her to wonder and she decided to seek out the truth.

One summer day she hid herself in the woods near the glade where her husband was wont to rest during the noonday heat. And as she had been told, she heard her husband's voice and these were the words he spoke: "Oh Aura, come to me as always and cool my fevered brow. Bring me relief from this heat which consumes me." And now poor Procris did believe what her own ears had heard, and sure that her husband was making love to a nymph, she fell fainting to the ground. Cephalus heard the rustle of leaves and, thinking it was some wild beast, threw his spear. He rushed to the spot only to find his wife vainly trying to draw the magic javelin from her breast. The heartbroken boy sought to ease her hurt and tend the ugly wound. But all was in vain. With her last breath, the dying girl begged, "Please, do not let Aura share the love I bore you. Don't take her for wife or lover!"

Then Cephalus understood and explained that Aura was only a harmless breeze. The expression of pain vanished at once and as Procris closed her eyes for the last time, there was a look of happiness and contentment on her face (Plate 24).

Echo and Narcissus

Cephisus, god of a winding stream, ensnared the nymph Liriope as she was bathing in his river. Of their love was born a child of extraordinary beauty, who was given the name of Narcissus. By the time he was sixteen, such was his perfection of face and form that nymphs and maidens pursued him.

One day, as Narcissus was hunting in the forest, he was spied by the nymph Echo, she who could not speak at any length, but had only the gift of repeating the last words she had heard. This affliction she suffered because of the offense she had given Juno. It happened in this manner. As we know, Jupiter on occasion would descend from Olympus to sport with playful nymphs in some hidden sylvan glade. Ever watchful, Juno would search for her errant husband and when Echo saw her approach, she would engage the goddess in such idle, beguiling talk that Jove had the opportunity to be warned and the nymphs to find shelter.

When Juno finally realized how she had been victimized, she exclaimed in her wrath, "That tongue of yours shall never again wag so freely!"

And now Echo could do no more than repeat the last words she heard. Otherwise, the once garrulous girl was speechless.

We take up our tale now where unfortunate Echo encountered Narcissus wandering through the woodland. She fell deeply in love with the lad at once, but had no power to speak her mind. Once, when he called aloud to a friend who had strayed, "Will you come," Echo answered, "Come!" He continued to call out, only to be astounded by the same curious reply. Finally, Echo came forth from behind a tree and sought to embrace Narcissus. But he fled her embrace as Daphne had fled the god Apollo.

The nymph was cruelly hurt by this rebuff and henceforth sought the seclusion of desolate caves. Her love did not lessen and she wasted away with grief and complaint until nothing remained of her body

(Plate 22). Only her plaintive voice continued to haunt woodland and countryside.

Narcissus spurned not only poor Echo, but all who sought his company and love. The goddess Nemesis one day granted the prayer of one of his scorned lovers. "Let Narcissus love only himself and never find respite from his sorrow!"

And thus it came to pass. One day the boy saw his own reflection in a quiet pool of silvery water. As he stretched himself at the stream's edge to drink of the clear water, he fell madly in love with the image that looked back at him. Pathetically enough, he admired and desired his very self. He tried in vain to kiss the reflection he saw. He sought again and again to clasp the ever elusive shape which vanished as soon as he dipped his anxious arms into the water. Neither eating nor sleeping, he suffered the cruelest pangs of unrequited love. He could not bring himself to leave the water's edge and soon came to pray for relief in death (Plate 19). Slowly he pined away. Towards the end, he looked fondly at the reflection in the pool and weakly called, "Farewell!" Echo, ever loving and ever watchful, faintly answered, "Farewell!" And so died the fair Narcissus. It is told that when the dryads, a band of wood-nymphs, prepared his funeral pyre and sought his body, it was nowhere to be found. Where last it had been, at the quiet water's edge, there was only a pale and lovely flower which to this day bears his name.

TWO TALES OF ADVENTURE

Van Dyck   *Art Gallery of Toronto*

DAEDALUS AND ICARUS

"I warn you, Icarus, to fly only the middle course"
(pp. 50, 51)

Plate 25

Plate 26

RESCUE OF ANDROMEDA
Perseus pierced the hide of the monster again and again (pp. 49, 56)

Piero di Cosimo
Uffizi, Florence

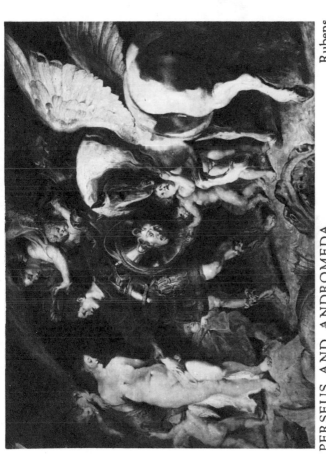

PERSEUS AND ANDROMEDA
Perseus advanced to liberate the maid (pp. 50, 56)

Rubens
Hermitage, Leningrad

Plate 27

Roman Painting from Pompeii *National Museum, Naples*

PERSEUS AND ANDROMEDA

He now led Andromeda ashore to her grateful parents
(pp. 49, 56)

Plate 28

CUPID AND PSYCHE

Raphael and his School   *Farnesina Palace, Rome*

CUPID SHOWS PSYCHE
TO THE THREE GRACES
(*p. 59*)

Plate 29

Raphael and his School   *Farnesina Palace, Rome*

VENUS ORDERS CUPID
TO SHOOT HIS ARROW AT PSYCHE
(*p. 59*)

Plate 30

Raphael and his School   *Farnesina Palace, Rome*

VENUS APPEARS
BEFORE JUPITER FOR AID
(*p. 59*)

Plate 31

Raphael and his School   *Farnesina Palace, Rome*

PSYCHE BRINGS
THE BEAUTY OINTMENT TO VENUS
(p. 59)

Plate 32

Raphael and his School   *Farnesina Palace, Rome*

JUNO AND CERES
PLEAD PSYCHE'S CAUSE WITH VENUS
(*p. 59*)

Plate 33

Raphael and his School   *Farnesina Palace. Rome*

MERCURY CONDUCTS PSYCHE
TO OLYMPUS
(*p. 59*)

Plate 34

THE QUEST FOR THE GOLDEN FLEECE

Follower of Pesellino

Metropolitan Museum of Art,
New York

THE CALYDONIAN BOAR HUNT

An episode in the life of Jason—
the hunting of the Calydonian Boar (p. 69)
[DETAIL]

Plate 35

Follower of Pesellino

JASON AND THE ARGONAUTS:

Plates 36-37

Scenes from the adventures of Jason and the Argonauts
(p. 69)

Plates 36-37

Follower of Pesellino   *Metropolitan Museum of Art, New York*

JASON LEAVES AEETES
TO PERFORM HIS TASKS
(p. 69)

[DETAIL]

Plate 38

Follower of Pesellino   *Metropolitan Museum of Art, New York*

[BACKGROUND]
JASON YOKES THE BRAZEN BULLS
AND SLAYS THE ARMED MEN
(*p. 69*)

[FOREGROUND]
KING AEETES AND COURTIERS
[DETAIL]

Plate 39

Delacroix   *Louvre, Paris*

MEDEA AND HER CHILDREN

*Medea, in her sorrow
and madness, slew her own children (pp. 69, 80)*

Plate 40

We come now to the telling of two tales which have enjoyed great popularity from the days when they were first told, well down to the present.

There are three paintings to illustrate the Perseus story. The earliest is by an unknown Roman painter of Pompeii. It is noble in concept and full of true classic restraint. Andromeda is being helped down from the rock by her liberator, who holds the head of Medusa in his left hand. It is surely a tribute to the genius of these ancient painters that some time before the year 79 A.D., such economical, straightforward representations were not isolated phenomena, but characterized an entire school of painting (Plate 28).

Piero di Cosimo, painter of Florence, is himself a character straight from the pages of myth, and his version of the Perseus story is a fanciful one indeed (Plate 26).

Peter Paul Rubens, more than most painters of his time, took both ideas and inspiration from the classics. He, too, has rendered the same story and through an examination of the three pictures we are afforded an

49

excellent opportunity to compare the interpretations of men of different temperaments, different epochs and varying talents (Plate 27).

In his representation of Daedalus and Icarus the Flemish master, Anthony Van Dyck, has selected that moment when the older and wiser man warns his son that when he takes off in flight, he should be sure not to mount too close to the sun. The following story will tell us what happened to the youth here pictured (Plate 25).

The Tale of Daedalus and Icarus

Daedalus was a native of Athens and had the reputation of being the greatest artist of his day. He was a skilled architect and sculptor and was besides a great inventor.

He had a nephew, Talus by name, whom he had trained and tutored and the pupil soon surpassed the master. As the boy's skill grew, so did envy in the heart of Daedalus. The envy grew to hate and one day the overwrought teacher killed the boy and buried his body. His crime was discovered and he was tried and found guilty.

Thereupon Daedalus fled Athens and arrived finally on the island of Crete, where King Minos held sway. The king welcomed him gladly, for he had need of his help.

But eventually Minos became distrustful of Daedalus and kept him prisoner on his island kingdom. The restless inventor soon hungered for the sight of other lands and most of all, his native city of Athens. And he thought to himself, "The king may block my escape by land and by water, but the sky above is open and in this way will I find freedom!"

Then he called to his side his young son, Icarus, and together they conceived a daring plan. From the wings of many birds they painfully gathered feathers of varying sizes and these, with twine and wax, they fashioned into huge wings very like the wings of real birds. The young Icarus helped as best he could, but he was of tender age and playful and frivolous and knew not the full import of what his father planned.

When the work was done, Daedalus secured the wings to his own body and that of the youth and painfully taught him how, by fluttering these, he could lift his body in flight. And then when he was skilled in this unhuman craft, Daedalus addressed his son.

"I warn you, Icarus, to fly only the middle course. If you venture too near the seas, the damp from the waters will weigh down your wings, and if you fly too high, the sun's fires will burn you" (Plate 25).

Then, with foreboding, and tears in his eyes, he fitted the wings for the last time to the boy's shoulders.

Soon young Icarus, joyful in his new-found prowess, left the middle path and winged his way higher and higher. The hot rays of the sun soon softened the wax which held the feathers together. And all at once, the fear-struck boy was flapping naked arms from which the wings had fallen and more rapidly than they, he fell into the deep blue sea.

The heartsick father called vainly, "Icarus, Icarus, where are you?" But the only traces of his boy were the varicolored feathers which floated gently on the surface of the water.

The Adventures of Perseus

You will recall that young Perseus, born to Danaë, was washed ashore with his mother on a small island, where they were befriended by the fisherman Dictys. You will recall, too, that the beauty of Danaë had once inflamed Jupiter himself with love. So it is small wonder that the ruler of the island kingdom, when he had seen Danaë, should have fallen in love with, and desired her. But for Perseus he had no use and bethought himself of a way to be rid of him.

One day he let it be known that he was to be married and ordered a huge celebration to which many were invited. Now it was the custom for all the guests to bring a lavish gift, but when it came time for Perseus to announce his offering, he stood abashed, for he had not known of this convention and had come empty-handed. He stood up proudly then and said, "No gift do I bring, O King, but if there is aught on this earth that you desire that may be had through zeal or daring—that thing will I bring to you!"

The king smiled benignly on the lad and inwardly

gloated. Then, in measured tones he said, "Bring me, if you would make good your boast, the head of Medusa!"

All the assembled guests were silent and awed, for they knew now that the king bore Perseus no good will. None had seen the face of Medusa and survived, for to look on her countenance was to be changed at once into stone. Perseus was being sent to his death.

The boy knew now how overbold he had been, but unabashed he addressed the king.

"O Polydectes, I leave at once these pleasant shores of Seriphus and I will not return until I bring with me the gift you crave."

But now that he had spoken so rashly, Perseus wandered to a high cliff to be alone and gather his thoughts. He was too proud to return to the king to ask release from his promise.

As he stood, lost in darkest thought, he discovered that two figures were close by. By their attributes, he recognized them at once, for the man with winged sandals was Hermes and the majestic woman was none other than Athena. Then the goddess addressed him, "O foolish and brave Perseus! You were tricked into a rash promise by the wily Polydectes. But with our help, you will slay Medusa and confound this king!"

Then Hermes said, "You may have my sandals and they will carry you with the wind's speed to your destination. And my sword you may take to slay Medusa." And Athena spoke up, too, and said, "Take my shield and when you encounter her who would

53

change you into stone, gaze not upon her directly, but use this polished shield as a mirror to guide your death-giving stroke."

First, with the aid of his borrowed sandals, Perseus flew northward, to where there lived the three Gray Women. He was told by Athena that they must help him in his quest.

The three Gray Women had but a single eye, which they shared amongst them. They passed it from one to the other and took their turns in viewing the bleak world which they inhabited. Perseus approached quietly and just as the eye was being passed, he snatched it from the hands of one of the women. Now they were helpless. Perseus then told of what he had done and in their plight they could do naught but direct him to the Garden of the Hesperides. Here there lived, as guardian of a tree on which golden apples grew, a band of nymphs, daughters of the giant Atlas. On his arrival he told them of his quest and how he sought Medusa's head.

The nymphs, already enamored of the fair youth, explained that he needed another aid for his gruesome task, the Cap of Darkness, a magic cap which rendered its wearer invisible. But this wonderful head-gear was to be had only by making a trip to the frightful underworld of Hades. One of the nymphs performed this difficult task for Perseus and he thereupon continued on his mission.

The winged sandals carried him towards his goal. He came finally to a drear and mournful landscape and, flying downward, he saw forms in stone which once had been men and animals, and he knew that he was close to that foul head which transformed all that beheld it. Looking now only at the shield, he watched the passing reflections which its shining surface mirrored. And then, suddenly, he came upon the Gorgons. They lay asleep and even in slumber they were horrible to behold. Only the face of one was of great beauty and for this reason she was more dreadful to look upon. She had claws like those of a baneful vulture and scales on her body like those of a monstrous sea-serpent. And where her hair should have been soft and lustrous and beautiful, there were instead vicious snakes which hissed and writhed and spat their venom at all intruders.

Then Perseus waited no longer. Looking only at the shield's reflection, he unsheathed his sword and smote with strength and skill. The head of Medusa rolled from its evil body and the hero wrapped it quickly in a goatskin he had brought with him and winged aloft.

He passed over many lands and unknown seas. As he gazed earthward, he saw a strange spectacle. Lashed to a rock with heavy chains, was the unclad figure of a young girl. Her body seemed like a fine marble carved by some skilled sculptor and it was white and lovely against the dark of the rock. As Perseus approached, she looked upwards at him with fear and shame and would have covered her nakedness had she been free to do so. Only her long golden hair offered some protection. In an instant, the youth was smitten with love at the sight of so much beauty. He alighted near her and bade her describe the events which had led to so sad a plight. Tearfully, and with sobbing voice, Andromeda, for this was the girl's name, related how her mother had boasted of the maid's beauty, and compared it all too favorably with the immortal loveliness of one of the sea deities. This offense caused a monster to be sent to ravage the land and to feed upon its inhabitants. An oracle was consulted and told them that only by sacrificing the fair Andromeda to the jaws of the frightful beast, could the land and its people be saved from further suffering. Brokenhearted, King Cepheus saw his daughter chained to the rock for this awful sacrifice. Perseus at once addressed the frenzied parents and asked if the girl could not be his for a bride if he would release her from chains and monster. Gladly they pledged her to him.

No sooner was the promise given than out of the sea there rose a creature of such malignant shape that it does not bear description. Forthwith, it sought to attack Perseus, who hovered protectingly before the maid. The young hero, fortified with the sword of Mercury, pierced the hide of his enemy again and again (Plate 26). As the monstrous shape sank below the waves, Perseus, with a single stroke, cut through the iron fetters and Andromeda fell into his waiting arms (Plates 27, 28).

After Perseus had made proper sacrifice to the gods,

he claimed his prize and amidst much rejoicing, the marriage feast was prepared.

Suddenly, the air was rent with the cries of angry men, and Phineus, brother of the king and uncle to the maid, Andromeda, came with his men to demand his bride—for to him had Andromeda been promised in marriage, before this evil befell the kingdom of Cepheus. Vainly did the king argue that Phineus should have come sooner and himself sought to save the girl from her horrible death. But Phineus listened not, and loosed his spear directly at Perseus, hoping to kill him at once and end all argument. However, the spear did not find its mark. Perseus now realized that he and his supporters were outnumbered by the angry warriors who threatened them. Suddenly, he called out, "Let all who are my friends turn their faces!" and so doing himself, he uncovered the Gorgon's head and held it in front of him. The onrushing figures were then frozen in their tracks and where a moment before there had been men of flesh and blood, there were now only statues of stone with spears upraised and angry scowls on their faces.

Now at last, the ceremony was joyfully continued and Perseus was wed to fair Andromeda. For an all too brief span, the married couple enjoyed one another, until Perseus remembered the reason for his journey. Taking his new bride with him, he returned to Seriphus to confront Polydectes and declare his mission accomplished. When Perseus came before the king and announced that he had brought back the head of Medusa, even then the king did not believe and called it all a lie. Then Perseus once again called out to his assembled friends, "Protect your eyes!" And again, he uncovered the head and held it before him for the king to see. The sightless eyes of Polydectes stared back at him. Thus was justice done and Danaë and her son avenged.

I HAVE USED as a source for the tale of Cupid and Psyche, the *Metamorphoses* or *Golden Ass* of Lucius Apuleius, as it was translated from the Latin by William Adlington in 1566. The original work was probably written during the middle of the second century A.D.

To illustrate this story, I have chosen the frescoes credited to Raphael and his assistants. Here is one of the rare instances in which a mythological tale is treated in a heroic manner by one of the great masters.

The paintings were conceived by Raphael quite late in his short career. He had already studied the heroic style of Michelangelo and seen the scientific investigations of Leonardo da Vinci. But most of all, he was affected by the passionate love for the newly-discovered examples of classical sculpture which were being excavated at the time in Rome and its environs. Much of his feeling for, and knowledge of, antique forms, were based on the new discoveries. All his new learning he poured into the designing of these pictures dealing with gods and goddesses (Plates 29, 30, 31, 32, 33, 34).

The Tale of Cupid and Psyche

Long ago during that time when gods and mortals mingled, there was a king whose wife bore him three daughters. Whereas two were of such exceeding beauty that the poets could hardly find the words with which to recount their comeliness, the third, who was named Psyche, boasted a beauty that defied description.

People came from distant places to see her and fell in worship before her as though she were the very goddess of love. And these travelers from afar came as to a shrine and having seen for themselves the wonder which was Psyche, they became contemptuous of Venus herself and neglected her altars and no longer made sacrifices to her.

So when the tongues of gods and goddesses began to wag and the insult was made plain to the mother of Cupid, she rose up in terrible wrath and planned a cruel revenge on this mortal.

She thereupon called to her side her prank-loving son Cupid and pointed out Psyche to him. "Go," she said, "and pierce with your arrow the all too proud and lovely breast of that boastful girl. Make her fall in love with the most vile and miserable creature that you can find on the earth below." Cupid took up his bow and quiver, winged earthward, had one look at Psyche and was lost. No victim of his gold arrows was more deeply in love than he.

Now it often happens with girls of such awesome beauty that men look upon them with longing and desire but are fearful to express, or make plain their sentiments. While Psyche remained a virgin, her two sisters albeit less lovely to behold won lovers and husbands for themselves. So Psyche lamented her celibate life and came soon to despise her own beauty.

Psyche's father began to suspect that this was the work of some unfriendly god or goddess and went himself to the nearby town of Miletus to consult the oracle of Apollo. The words he heard were terrifying ones. Psyche was to be dressed in clothes of mourning, taken to a neighboring mountain and left there for the approach of her lover and future husband. And he, in the words of the oracle, would prove to be no fair youth of godlike splendor but a dire and fierce winged serpent who haunted the starry skies.

So the sad parents prepared this funereal marriage for their unfortunate daughter. All the people of the town mourned and wept and Psyche was escorted to the appointed place and left to her fate.

But as Psyche stood alone on the mountain peak, gentle Zephyrus, servant of Cupid, picked her up and carried her tenderly from the cold pinnacle to a pleasant, scented valley far below.

For a while she slept and then awakened refreshed and inquisitive. In the distance she saw a magnificent edifice and hastened towards it. It seemed built not by the hand of man but by some godly artificer.

Cautiously Psyche ventured into this building and

saw that it was unguarded and uninhabited. Suddenly she heard a voice, which like that of the poor nymph Echo seemed to boast no body or earthly shape. "All this belongs to you, Psyche," the voice said. "Come bathe and refresh your tired limbs and prepare for dinner. We are here quite near but invisible and will minister gladly to your every whim and desire."

All was done as the voice promised and Psyche was served not as a mortal but more like one of the most privileged of goddesses. At night she went to bed with beating heart and a mixture of such expectations and fears as are proper for a young virgin lying in her marriage bed.

Then her husband came and remained invisible all through the night. With the first dawn he was gone, leaving the new bride to wonder at her strange but not unhappy lot.

While Psyche's parents lamented the loss of their daughter, the two elder girls, being idle and curious, pondered the fate of their sister.

But after long days and nights had passed and Psyche had become accustomed to a life of luxury, and the all too brief period of love in her husband's arms, she became bored and restless. One night she begged her husband to be permitted to visit with her sisters. Reluctantly Cupid consented but again warned her not to discuss him or the nature of their life together.

When the sisters came to the peak where Psyche had last been seen, Cupid's servant Zephyrus lifted them gently and set them down to rest unhurt in the valley where Psyche was so richly housed. Psyche led the girls to her home and they were entertained in a manner suited to residents of Olympus. Soon they asked the inevitable question of Psyche. What was her husband like? Remembering her promise, she spoke in vaguest terms and described him as a comely, beardless lad, who spent his days away from home hunting in the hills and fishing in the nearby streams.

Then Psyche gave them magnificent gifts and called to Zephyrus to carry them back whence they came.

But these sisters were envious and jealous and above all curious. They decided to see their sister once again and ferret out her secret.

Cupid, of course, knew of their plans and warned his bride that if the sisters came again and suggested to her that she try and see her husband's face, she must be firm and yield not to the temptation.

But Psyche begged to be allowed once more to see her sisters. And during that night, such were her blandishments and the honey of her words, that he agreed—much against his better judgment.

Now this time, after having been lavishly entertained, the sisters questioned Psyche again about the appearance of her husband and soon frightened her in the following manner. They recalled the oracle of Apollo and convinced her that, as had been prophesied, she was married to, and lying with, not a young god, but a serpentine monster of horrible appearance and evil intent. They suggested that she fortify herself with a sharp blade and a lantern and when her husband was sound asleep to see for herself. If he was indeed what they had heard, she could forthwith cut off his head and free herself from this horrible bondage.

That very night she did as had been suggested and when her husband was in a deep sleep, she took her oil lamp and the whetted blade and looked in the bed. What she saw was hardly a monster, but rather the most beautiful of young men, one worthy to compete with Psyche herself in fairness. All atremble, she fell to her knees seeking to hide her shameful act. Some drops of oil fell on Cupid's shoulder and the pain awakened him. Without a word of farewell he disappeared, leaving the anguished girl to consider her misdeed and her sad fate.

Meanwhile Venus had learned of her son's injury, and, rushing back to her golden chamber, she found the lad wounded and in distress. First she reproached him for his deception, but soon in motherly fashion she tried to assuage his pain.

When Cupid was well on his way to recovery, Venus left the bedchamber and shortly after encountered Juno and Ceres. The two goddesses knew all that had happened and tried to dim the fury of her anger.

Psyche decided in her despair to throw herself on the mercy of the irate goddess. The girl begged forgiveness and offered to do penance of any sort to pay for her crime.

Venus thereupon threw on the ground a great quantity of seeds of different varieties. There were millet and barley and poppy and beans and others, all differing in size and color. She ordered Psyche to sort these into separate piles within the day else her punishment would be immediate and severe.

There is a creature of good heart called sometimes ant and sometimes pismire. One of this industrious breed observed the sad state of Psyche and became indignant at the injustice of Venus. He called at once to his brothers, and these six-footed creatures came in hosts, lined up wave after wave as if for battle. Before nightfall the grains were arranged in separate piles and the brave ants returned whence they had come.

Venus raged when she saw her first task accomplished and called Psyche to her side. "Look in the valley below," she ordered. "There are sheep grazing with fleece of gold. Go forthwith and bring to me some of the wool from their backs."

Psyche knew this to be an evil ruse and thought to end her sorrow by drowning herself in a nearby stream. But a voice spoke to her from the water, "Do not yet give up hope, fair Psyche. The sheep below are fiendish and would kill you I know, but go when the sun is set and the flock is resting. At your ease, and in all safety, you may pick the golden fleece from the briars to which strands have clung."

So Psyche went and gathered up the locks of seeming gold and took them to Venus.

This time the goddess in her hypocrisy pretended to laugh and be glad. "I will test your courage, Psyche," she said. "Go to the stream which tumbles from the mountain peak yonder and bring some of its black water to me in this vessel." Psyche took the crystal bottle and set off once more. Now the eagle of almighty Jupiter himself came to her aid. In his beak he took the bottle, held it in the falling stream until it was filled, and placed it quickly in the girl's anxious hands.

Psyche returned to Venus and joyfully presented the vessel. But the angry goddess spoke in cruel tones again. "One duty more remains to be completed before you may atone for your sins. Go now to Hades and seek out Proserpina. Take this box and have her put in it some small portion of her beauty. I need only enough to supply me for one day."

Again Psyche thought to throw herself from the rocks and make an end to all her earthly torture. But when she climbed to a high peak a voice addressed her and gave her full directions for descending unharmed to the black regions of Death. "Go directly to Proserpina," the voice continued, "and she will be gracious and fill your box. But as you return to Venus with it, be sure not to remove the lid. Remember Pandora and the evil which befell her."

Alas, Psyche was neither the first nor the last maiden with vanity or curiosity. "Why should I not take the smallest bit of this divine beauty for my own face." She opened the box then and found no beauty salve; but a mist arose from the inside and caused her to fall into a deathlike sleep.

Cupid was recovered from his wound caused by the drops of oil, and had gone in search of his beloved.

He found her where she had fallen. After clearing the sleep from her brain and refilling the box, he quickly took flight and left Psyche with no memory of what had occurred. She continued on her way and brought to Venus the present she had demanded.

Cupid, fearing the wrath of his mother, went himself before Jupiter to plead his cause. Then the leader of all the celestial powers commanded Mercury to convoke the gods and goddesses and Jupiter made an eloquent plea for Cupid. Mercury was dispatched again, to bring Psyche to the palace of heaven. When she had arrived Jupiter held out a cup to her and said, "Drink, Psyche, of this divine liquid of immortality that you may forever and ever be united with Cupid in joyous and fruitful matrimony."

In due time Psyche bore a child who was given the name of Pleasure.

THE STORY OF Jason's many adventures while in pursuit of the famed Golden Fleece was popular from a very early date. For excitement and variety of incident it ranks second to no other tale. This voyage supposedly took place some time before the Trojan War and before Ulysses experienced similar difficulties and surprises while attempting to return home after the sack of Troy.

The story of the Argonauts appealed to many writers, and in verse and prose the tale has been retold from the time of Pindar in the sixth century B.C., down to William Morris in the nineteenth century, and Robert Graves in our own time.

In our present account we have followed the most famous version, written by Apollonius of Rhodes, under the title *The Argonautica*. His exact dates are not known but he probably lived and wrote during the third century B.C.

Popular though the story of the Argonauts proved to be, there are comparatively few instances of its depiction in paintings by well-known artists. The pictures here reproduced are details from two panels generally ascribed to a follower of Pesellino, a fifteenth century Florentine master. The panels were probably parts of *cassones* or marriage chests.

The Florentine painter handled the story of Jason and his followers as though it were a fairy tale. It is painted in what is known as the continuous style, where the same character appears repeatedly in the picture, playing his part in various episodes of the story (Plates 35, 36-37, 38, 39).

Here, then, is a challenge for the reader. Like a fifteenth century Florentine seeing these panels for the first time, he will fit picture to story and let them complete and enhance one another.

Four centuries after the follower of Pesellino dealt with the story of Jason's adventures, the French romantic painter, Eugene Delacroix, painted a canvas of Medea and her children. His inspiration must certainly have come from the drama of Euripides, an unforgettable study of disillusioned love in which the climax is reached when Medea slays her children (Plate 40).

Jason and the Quest for the Golden Fleece

Long ago Athamas and Nephele reigned as king and queen of Thessaly. In the first happy years of their union, they had two children, Helle, a girl, and Phryxus, a boy.

When Athamas no longer loved his queen, but lavished attentions on another, the anxious mother feared for the welfare of her children and planned to send them far away to a safe land. Mercury came to help her and supplied a ram with fleece of gold, that had the power to fly through the air. Phryxus and Helle mounted the ram and began their fateful journey. As they passed over a body of water, Helle became dizzy from looking down, and fell into the sea, where she was drowned. In memory of her, this strait was for long known as the Hellespont.

Phryxus finally came safely to the kingdom of Colchis and was well received by King Aeetes. The ram was sacrificed to Jupiter and the golden fleece hidden in a quiet grove, where it was guarded by an ever watchful dragon.

Adjacent to Thessaly, there was a kingdom, ruled over by Aeson, father of Jason, the hero of our tale. When Aeson tired of the duties of kingship, he gave over the crown to his brother, Pelias, on condition that when Jason came of age he should receive it back. But Pelias, unlike his brother, seemed not to weary of wearing a crown and when Jason came to demand his kingdom, Pelias made the following suggestion: "Let the youth first try himself by a bold adventure!"

Then Jason, being fearless and restless too, with great spirit undertook the quest.

The Preparation

A ship of finest construction was made ready by Argus. There was room in it for fifty men, and so wonderful was the craft displayed in its making that in honor of its builder it was named the Argo.

Then, in answer to Jason's call to adventure, there came men from various parts of the kingdom and they were of diverse origins and pedigrees. Mortals mingled with gods and demigods. Among them too, was the most powerful man in all Greece, Hercules himself.

When all was in readiness, the townsfolk came down to see the wonderful ship and the heroes who would man it. Then, while Orpheus sang to music of his own making, the Argo was launched and the shouts of the warriors on board mingled with the cries and last words of advice of those left on the shore. The rowers bent to the oars and the voyage of the Argo had begun.

Then one day, when the sea was calm, an island was

sighted, and with renewed vigor and high spirits the men pointed the prow shoreward. In no time, the Argo's bottom scraped the sandy beach of the island of Lemnos.

Hypsipyle and the Women of Lemnos

In earlier days, the men who inhabited the island had gone off to war in Thrace and had brought back only the women and maids as captives. For these, they developed so strong a passion that they rejected their own wives and the young girls who had so patiently awaited their return. So strong and urgent was their love for these foreign women that they forgot to make the usual sacrifices to Venus. The wrath of the goddess was great, indeed. She roused the native women of Lemnos to such a heat of resentment, it is said, that they armed themselves and slew not only all of the captives, but all the men and boys who had once been their husbands and loved ones. These women then donned armor and learned to plow the fields and do all the work of men.

Jason had sent a herald ashore to indicate his friendly intentions, for the Argonauts knew not of what had happened earlier on this unhappy isle. An old woman then rose up in an assembly that had been called by the queen and declared that the invaders should not be bribed to go away, as had been suggested by some, but invited to the island as guests. She pointed around her to gray-haired virgins and related how plainly was their painful destiny written.

This speech was received with great satisfaction by those assembled and Hypsipyle forthwith sent a messenger to bid Jason and his men land at once and enter the friendly city.

Briefly Hypsipyle told the story of the island, not without blushes as she looked longingly at Jason. She invited the Argonauts to stay on the island and to their leader she made offer of kingship.

Then, in this once quiet city, there was dancing and merrymaking and all the proper sacrifices were made to the gods. Only Hercules and a few companions stayed on board the Argo. Day after day, the ship remained anchored in this happy port and the sailing was repeatedly delayed.

One day, Hercules in anger addressed the men. "Is this the way to win fame?" he asked. "To plow the fields for foreign women by day and make love to them at night! Did we set sail only to re-stock this island, or to bring back the Golden Fleece from far-away Colchis? We have made a pledge and the people at home await us! Let us lift the sails again and ply the oars and be on our way!" And all knew that he spoke wisely and quickly made themselves ready for departure.

Then Hypsipyle and her women came down to the shoreline to say their farewells. And as before, there were sighs and tears and the queen bade Jason a safe journey and a safe return, but in her heart she knew that she was destined never again to see her lover.

Then the hawsers were loosed and the ship pushed out from the shallows. The men took up their oars again and smote the waves. The Argo was once more on its way.

The Fight of Polydeuces and Amycus

When land was again sighted, the men quickly dropped anchor and went ashore. Now this was the kingdom of Amycus, a proud and boastful king, who ruled over a people called the Bebrycians. He had made an ordinance that if strangers came to his land, they might not depart unless one of their number met the king himself in a boxing match. So, when the Argonauts landed, Amycus and his subjects met them on the beach and in a belligerent tone the king announced, "Select your bravest fighter to meet me in a boxing match!" So arrogant was Amycus in his assurance of quick victory, that Polydeuces stepped forth from the ranks of the Argonauts and said simply, "I will meet you!"

Then a place was cleared and the fighters made ready, while the men sat in separate groups to watch the match.

Now Amycus was tall and powerful, having almost the physique of a giant, while Polydeuces was smaller in stature but ideally formed, and a true master of the art of boxing. With a smile on his lips, he confidently picked up his gloves, which were quickly laced.

The fight began at once and so nimble and clever was the Argonaut that Amycus reached him with few blows. None the less, many fierce blows were landed by both fighters, who panted and sweated like angry bulls. At last, Polydeuces slipped in under a powerful blow by his rival and struck him with all his might, just above the ear and broke all the bones. Amycus, in agony, fell to his knees and as the Argonauts in unison gave out a cry of victory, he gasped out his final breath.

Then the Bebyricians rushed at the invaders, but were met by drawn swords. The battle was short, for the Argonauts, gloating over the victory of Polydeuces, put the foe to rout and after caring for their wounded, returned to the ship and sailed away from this sorry land.

King Phineus and the Harpies

Now the boat approached next the shores of Thrace, where Phineus was king. The Argonauts were welcomed and brought as guests to his palace. When they were all assembled in his huge banquet hall, Phineus told of his affliction.

"As you see," he began, "I am blind and old and weak and barely with the strength to speak. This is punishment for a horrible thing I did once in the years gone by. You will see in a moment the terrible nature of my torment."

As he spoke, the food was being brought to the banquet tables, but before the king or his guests had the chance to bring it to their mouths, a fluttering of many wings was heard and with the wind's speed, a band of Harpies flew into the hall. These were part woman and part vulture, with the head and breasts of the former and the wings and claws of the latter. Quickly these revolting creatures snatched the food from the hands of all assembled and befouled whatever was left on the tables. No human could now partake of the noisome mess which they left. Only a few morsels remained, so that the tormented king might not find release in death from hunger.

Suddenly, Zetes and Calais, who were children of the North Wind, and endowed with the ability to fly through space, rose from their seats and pursued the Harpies. Soon they overtook them and would indeed have slain them all, had they not been told by a divine voice that these Harpies were the Hounds of Jupiter and should not be killed. The same voice promised that the Harpies would never again plague the blind king. The banquet continued amid rejoicing and Phineus told the Argonauts what they needed to know, the eastward route to Colchis. And he warned them about the danger of the Clashing Rocks called the Symplegades and how to pass by them safely.

Whenever an unsuspecting mariner guided his boat between these huge rocks, they rushed together with so terrible a force that nothing could survive. Phineus told the Argonauts to release a dove when they approached this spot and if the dove flew safely between the rocks, this was to be taken as a good omen that the Argo might sail through. The dove flew through the opening, losing only one tail feather, as the rocks crashed. The men cheered and pulled on the oars as the rocks separated. On the crest of a huge wave, they safely passed by this danger. And then, finally, the shores of Colchis were in sight and they could see in the distance the palace of Aeetes.

The Golden Fleece

Not knowing of their quest, Aeetes invited the bold adventurers to his palace and after they had supped lavishly, Jason arose and told the story of their voyage and its purpose. The king tried to conceal his anger and made the following offer to Jason:

"You have come on a long and perilous journey and have performed many deeds of valor and for these feats of daring we salute you, O worthy Argonauts.

But we too, prize the Fleece of Gold which hangs in yonder sacred grove. This treasure we will yield to you gladly, however, if a few tasks are fulfilled by one of your brave band. First, there are two bulls with legs of bronze and these animals breathe fire from their nostrils. They must be yoked and made to plow a field which I will select. Then you must take some seeds which I have in my possession and sow them rapidly in the furrows. The crop will be a strange one, for warriors of fearsome mien will grow out of the ground. These you must slay without help from your own men. If all this is accomplished, then the Golden Fleece will be yours and you may carry it safely back across the seas to the land from which you sailed."

Now Jason knew that there was guile behind the king's words; and with fear in his heart, but a confident smile on his face, he rose up and answered King Aeetes, "I, Jason, pledge myself to do these things!"

Now Medea, the daughter of Aeetes, was schooled in witchcraft, and mistress of divers magical accomplishments. At their first meeting, she fell in love with Jason. On the eve of the fateful day, she approached him as he stood alone outside his camp and offered him her help. Jason was struck by her beauty and moved by her offer to make such great sacrifice for his sake. She gave him an ointment, with which he was to cover his body and his weapons. This would make him invulnerable. Neither the blows of an enemy, nor the fiery blasts from the brazen bulls could harm him.

78

Jason then clasped the fair princess in a strong embrace and pledged himself to take her with him as his wife as soon as the task was accomplished.

And now dawned the great day of trial for the Argonauts. They came to the field outside the city, where the test was to be made and already Aeetes and his subjects were assembled. Medea stood at her father's side and watched with pounding heart, as her new-found lover led the brave band of adventurers to the center of the field.

In a moment, the gate was opened and the two bulls, with legs of bronze, bellowing and breathing fire, rushed at Jason. He met their fierce onslaught and neither the power of their huge forms nor the fire which they breathed out could harm him. Quickly, he brought them to their knees, yoked them to the plow and, to the cheers of the Argonauts, plowed the field.

Then Jason sowed the dragon seeds, for such was their nature, and at once, hundreds of fully armed warriors grew out of the ground. As the Argonauts watched, they saw to their horror that some of these giants were already full-grown and no sooner freed from the earth than they were rushing towards their leader. Others, with heads or chests just emerging from the soil, would soon be ripe for battle.

But Jason remembered the advice of Medea. He picked up a huge stone and threw it in the midst of these warriors. Immediately, they turned from him and began to fight among themselves for possession of the useless boulder. In short order, they had slain

79

one another and Jason quickly killed the few who remained.

Then a cheer arose from the assembled spectators. But Jason did not go directly to Aeetes to claim his prize. By now he understood the real character of this deceitful king. But that night, when all were asleep, the Argo was made ready for a quick sailing. Then Jason hurried to the grove where the Fleece was hung and removed it from the tree.

Then once again, the Argo set sail. Medea stood sobbing in Jason's arms, as she looked for the last time on her native land.

Of Jason and Medea, there is more to tell, but it is not a good tale. I would prefer that you read of it elsewhere. Medea caused the death of her father and of her brother. Evil compounds evil, and in later years, after she had borne to Jason two sons, he left her bed for a younger and fairer maiden, daughter to another king.

If you must know of this great tragedy of disillusioned love, and of how Medea, in her sorrow and madness, slew her own children, there is a tale told by Euripides (Plate 40). I prefer, however, to leave off here. The Quest is over, and Jason, its hero, glorious in the full flower of young manhood and glorious in the accomplishment of a daring mission, is safe at last in his native land.

Pollaiuolo   *Uffizi, Florence*

HERCULES STRANGLING ANTAEUS

Hercules lifted his rival
from the ground and strangled him (pp. 82, 87) Plate 41

Pollaiuolo   *Uffizi, Florence*

HERCULES SLAYING THE HYDRA

He was sent to slay the Hydra of Lerna,
a serpent-like creature with nine heads (pp. 82, 84)

Plate 42

Reni   *Louvre, Paris*

HERCULES AND THE HYDRA OF LERNA

*As he cut off each head,
two grew in its place (pp. 82, 84)*

Plate 43

Roman Painting from Pompeii   *Casa D'Amantius,*
Pompeii

HERCULES IN
THE GARDEN OF THE HESPERIDES

*In the garden of the Hesperides
there was a tree which bore golden apples (pp. 82, 87)*

Plate 44

Gleyre   Neuchâtel Museum

HERCULES AND QUEEN OMPHALE

*She compelled him to do a woman's work
such as weaving and spinning (pp. 82, 88)*

Plate 45

RAPE OF DEIANIRA
or HERCULES AND NESSUS
Hercules shot an arrow at the centaur (pp. 82, 89)

Pollaiuolo
Art Gallery,
Yale University

Plate 46

THE TROJAN WAR

Rubens   *Dresden Museum*

THE JUDGMENT OF PARIS

There appeared before Paris
three goddesses of unbelievable beauty (p. 92)

Plate 47

PARIS AND HELEN
Paris was hospitably received by fair Helen (p. 92)

David
Louvre, Paris

Plate 48

Attributed to
Benozzo Gozzoli

THE RAPE OF HELEN

Paris carried Helen off to Troy (p. 92)

National Gallery,
London

Plate 49

Roman Painting from Pompeii   *National Museum, Naples*

THE SACRIFICE OF IPHIGENIA

*It was decided that Iphigenia, daughter of Agamemnon,
must be sacrificed (p. 93)*

Plate 50

Tiepolo   *Villa Valmarana, Vicenza*

BRISEIS BROUGHT BEFORE AGAMEMNON

*Agamemnon insisted that he have in exchange Briseis, a
beautiful young captive who had been earlier
awarded to Achilles (p. 93)*

Plate 51

Ingres

Aix en Provence Museum

JUPITER AND THETIS

*Thetis appears before Jupiter
to ask for help for her son, Achilles*

Plate 52

Tiepolo National Gallery, London

THE BUILDING OF THE TROJAN HORSE

Ulysses caused a huge wooden horse to be constructed (p. 96)

Plate 5

El Greco

THE LAOCOÖN

The serpents wound their terrible bodies around the group
and slowly strangled all life out of father and sons (p. 96)

Plate 54

David   Montpellier Museum

HECTOR

Hector was stripped of all armor and lay naked and exposed
(p. 95)

Plate 55

AJAX AND
CASSANDRA

*Cassandra, daughter of King Priam, was torn
from the altar where she had been praying*

Plate 56

Rubens

Liechtenstein Gallery, Vienna

CHAPTER VIII

THE ADVENTURES
OF HERCULES

IN THE FIGURE of Hercules, or Heracles, as he was known to the Greeks, we have truly a subject suited for the making of myths. Above all else, he was a symbol of strength and fearlessness. By most standards, he was certainly no ideal hero, for he was not overly bright, he was sensitive only on occasion, and he had an uncontrollable temper. Along with his good deeds, he caused much evil in the course of his life, and sought to compensate for his crimes by throwing himself into any adventure which offered danger and harm to his person. The Greeks loved him, for he was foolhardy in his daring and offered to fight with anyone, even the Immortals. Once, when the heat of the sun bothered him, he was ready to shoot his arrows at the Sun God, unless he got relief!

From the very beginning, he had great forces lined up against him, for Juno herself was his sworn enemy, and the cause of many of his troubles.

Hercules is perhaps best remembered for his performance of the famed twelve labors, but actually, he had many adventures before and after this sequence of undertakings.

Antonio Pollaiuolo, fifteenth century painter of Florence, has done two small but heroic panels, showing Hercules strangling Antaeus and slaying the Hydra (Plates 41, 42). About one hundred years later, Guido Reni, a painter of the High Renaissance in Italy, painted the same Hydra encounter, and it is interesting to compare the two versions (Plate 43).

An early Pompeian fresco, painted by some great artist doomed to anonymity, represents Hercules in the Garden of the Hesperides when he seeks the golden apples (Plate 44).

There is also a much later picture by Gleyre. Here, in an elaborately detailed setting of pseudo-classical architecture, Hercules is shown performing one of the womanly tasks set for him by Queen Omphale (Plate 45).

Lastly, there is a dramatic and highly poetic picture, also painted by Pollaiuolo, representing the slaying of Nessus, the Centaur, when he attempts to carry off Deianira, the bride of Hercules (Plate 46).

The Labors of Hercules

Almighty Jupiter one day beheld Alcmena, the wife of Amphitryon, and at once desired her. When the husband was away fighting a war, Jupiter transformed himself into the very shape and semblance of the absent Amphitryon. Alcmena, unaware, so it is alleged, of the deception, received him willingly. And of the union, Hercules was born. Alcmena, who had only recently bid farewell to her true husband, bore also to him a second son named Iphicles. Juno now nursed a deep hatred for Hercules.

One day, when the infants were asleep, Juno sent two huge serpents to strangle them in their sleep. But in the dead of night, when the monsters reared up to envelop the infants in their coils, the eight-month-old Hercules calmly reached out and grasped the frightful creatures just under the head, and crushed all life from their writhing bodies. When Amphitryon rushed into the room, he found the laughing infant holding two lifeless serpents in his chubby hands.

Hercules grew rapidly in stature and in strength and he developed early an uncontrollable temper. One day, when he was reprimanded for striking a false note on his lyre, he raised the instrument and struck his teacher with such force that he died at once.

One of the first worthy deeds of his adolescence was the slaying of a fierce lion that had decimated many herds and terrified the shepherds of this region. He next helped the natives of Thebes defeat a hated enemy and was rewarded by being given the lovely princess Megara in marriage. She bore him several beautiful children. Jealous of his good fortune, Juno sent a sudden madness to overtake him. Sitting with his family, Hercules suddenly saw them not as his loved ones but as wild animals. Springing up in a wild frenzy, he slew them all. Then he returned to his senses and knew what a monstrous thing he had done.

So great was his horror and sorrow that for a while he prowled the forests like a wild beast, and no man dared to come near him. He wandered until he came to Delphi, where he questioned the famed oracle as to how he might purge himself and become again cleansed and without shame. The oracle insisted that some penance must be done. It was ordained that he appear before his cousin, Eurystheus, king of Mycenae, and submit to his will, follow his directions and perform whatever labors he set him.

The initial labor was to slay the Nemean lion. When no arrow shot by Hercules would pierce its skin, and no clubbing subdue the monster, Hercules dropped all weapons and with his bare hands choked out its life. He slung the carcass over his shoulders and carried it to the palace of Eurystheus.

Next Hercules was sent to slay the Hydra of Lerna, a serpent-like creature with nine heads, one of which was immortal (Plate 42). In this task Hercules had his cousin, Iolaus, help him. As he cut off each head with fiercest strokes, two grew in its place (Plate 43). Then Iolaus, directed by his great cousin, heated a brand, and as Hercules chopped off each head, he seared the neck with the glowing brand and no new heads grew back. Over the last immortal head he rolled a huge rock and from under its prodigious weight, the Hydra has never escaped.

The third labor was to bring to the court the Cerynean stag, sacred to Athena. Hercules chased it for a whole year, and when it was worn with fatigue, cornered it, and with Athena's consent, brought it to Mycenae.

Now the fourth task given to Hercules was to master a wild boar which had its lair high in the mountains. Hercules pursued the beast relentlessly and when the snows finally fell, he was enabled to track the weary animal to its last hiding place, and capture it.

There was a King Augeas, who ruled over a fertile land, and had vast flocks of prize cattle. So numerous were his flocks and so few his servants, that his stables were never clean and the filth increased from year to year. Eurystheus gave Hercules the seemingly hopeless task of cleaning the stables in a single day. But Hercules diverted the courses of two swift-flowing streams so that they splashed their way through the Augean stables and cleansed in a single day the noisome filth of years.

Next, Hercules pitted himself against the Stymphalian birds, a strange and pestiferous breed, with claws of iron and quills sharp as a huntsman's arrow. Hercules took with him a huge shield for this labor. He rang a bell, which he also carried, beat a clamorous tattoo on the shield, and when the birds which had plagued the natives of Stymphalus loosed their murderous quills, they blunted their points on the huge protecting shield. Thus thwarted, the birds flew off, but not before Hercules brought down many with his own well-aimed arrows.

This brings us to the seventh labor, and Hercules to the island of Crete, whither he was sent to conquer the savage bull which was Poseidon's gift to King Minos. It was famed for a rare combination of strength and beauty. Hercules found the bull one day drinking from its favorite stream, and grasping the animal by the horns, wrestled with it and subdued it. Suddenly, after its conquest, all fierceness went out of the bull and it became gentle and willing to follow its new master.

As an eighth labor, Hercules was sent to conquer a pair of steeds belonging to King Diomedes. These fierce creatures fed only on human flesh. With his bare hands, Hercules brought them to their knees, and drove them off subdued and broken.

For his ninth task, Hercules was sent to the land of the Amazons, where the beautiful Queen Hippolyta reigned. Hercules was ordered to bring back the girdle of Hippolyta. Now the queen had heard of the wondrous exploits of Hercules, and willingly offered herself as well as the girdle. When Hippolyta came down to the sea to bid farewell to Hercules as he prepared to sail homeward, Juno spread the rumor in the city that Hercules and his companions were carrying off the queen. The Amazons attacked, and Hercules, all too easily aroused, suspected a plot and slew the innocent queen.

The tenth labor was to bring back to Mycenae the

cattle of the monstrous giant Geryon, he who had three bodies and heads and extra arms and legs and wings. As Hercules neared Geryon's domain, a mountain blocked his approach, which this time was by water. Then Hercules broke the mountain apart and pushed the two halves to either side, creating a narrow sea corridor, through which he sailed. The Pillars of Hercules, as they are called, still stand on either side of the strait of Gibraltar for everyone to see. Hercules soon arrived at his destination, slew Geryon and brought back the cattle to Mycenae.

In the garden of the Hesperides there was a tree which bore golden apples (Plate 44). An ever wakeful dragon helped guard the tree, and it was aided in this task by the Hesperides, fair nymphs who were the daughters of mighty Atlas. Eurystheus set as the eleventh task for Hercules the acquisition of these apples.

Hercules set forth to find the garden and encountered many difficulties on the way. I mention only a few, first his struggle with Antaeus, a wrestler almost as powerful as Hercules himself. Antaeus forbade passage unless the two first met in a test of strength. Now all of the challenger's strength derived from Earth, who was his mother, and each time that Hercules threw Antaeus to the ground, he sprang up with renewed energy. Then Hercules guessed his secret, and held him off the ground and strangled and killed him (Plate 41).

Hercules was then advised to go to Libya and induce Atlas to help him acquire the golden apples.

He told Atlas about the labor he was compelled to perform, and begged him to go and get the apples for him. Atlas replied, "This I will do, if you will relieve me of my burden while I am gone." Then Atlas carefully shifted the world from his own shoulders to those of Hercules. In spite of his care, buildings shook and fell down as the great globe trembled. When Atlas returned, having enjoyed his new-found freedom, he suggested that Hercules stay where he was, while he, Atlas, carried the apples to Eurystheus.

Hercules pretended to agree and asked only that Atlas hold the world for an instant, while he padded his shoulders with his lion skin, to ease the strain. Again they shifted the world, whereupon Hercules picked up the apples and left the puzzled giant to meditate on his error of judgment.

Now Hercules was forced to interrupt the performance of his Labors when he was punished by Jupiter for one of his fits of temper. He was sent as a slave to Queen Omphale in Lydia, where he served her for several years. She compelled him to dress often like a woman and do woman's work, such as weaving and spinning (Plate 45). At the end of his sentence, he was free again to live a man's life.

Hercules had finally to descend to the tenebrous and dreadful regions of the dead to bring back the triple-headed Cerberus. When Hercules finally encountered this creature, he quickly caught it by the throat and subdued it. He then appeared before Pluto to ask permission to carry the conquered monster to the upper world. This request Pluto granted and Hercules once again brought his quarry to the palace of Eurystheus and presented it to the king.

Hercules, about this time, was attracted by the beauty of Deianira, princess of Aetolia, who was also loved by the river god, Achelous. Hercules fought with the god and, as always, won his prize. As he was carrying her home, they came to a wide river. On its bank stood the Centaur, Nessus, who offered to carry the young bride on his back. Hercules agreed, but no sooner did Nessus reach the middle of the stream than he made advances to Deianira. She screamed in fright and Hercules, still on the shore, shot an arrow at the Centaur (Plate 46). When Nessus reached the other bank, he fell dying to the ground. With his last breath, he pretended to be contrite, and told the girl to take a scarf she was wearing and dip it in the blood flowing from his wound. Then he told Deianira that if Hercules should ever cease to love her, she was to extract the blood from this cloth and dip some garment of Hercules in the magic solution and his love for her was sure to return in all its early vigor.

Deianira guarded this love charm until one day she heard that her husband was enamored of the beautiful maiden Iole. She did now as Nessus had advised, and when Hercules put on the shirt which she had prepared, a poison began to burn deep into his body and the tortured giant knew now that he was dying. He ordered his friends to build a funeral pyre on Mount Oeta and hither they carried him. Here he lay himself down to die. The pyre was lighted and the flames leaped up to consume his pain-racked body. But the gods ordained that so worthy a hero should not die a mortal's death, and had Hercules carried to Olympus. Now that all his earthly labors were done, a life of peace and contentment finally awaited him.

Almost every schoolboy in every land knows something of the story of the Trojan War, a bloody conflict immortalized by the work of Homer. The Iliad was written some thousand years before Christ, and the Greek bard based his epic on what is probably one of the happiest blendings of fact and fiction.

This is the story of a great conflict which raged for all of ten years and might well have been avoided if the gods of Olympus had not slighted one of their own number. Eris was the goddess of Discord, and once when a banquet was given, she was not invited. When the merrymaking was at its height, Eris threw a golden apple into the dining hall, and it was marked for all to see with the legend, "For the Most Fair." Many claimed the prize, but finally three contestants remained. Venus was of course one, and Juno and Minerva contested her claim to be the most beautiful of the inhabitants of Olympus. Zeus suggested that the three contestants travel to Mount Ida, where young Paris, son of Priam, the king of Troy, was guarding some flocks for his father. He was an excellent judge of feminine beauty, Zeus insisted, and would award the apple fairly.

So one day as Paris was resting under a tree during the noonday's heat, there appeared before him three goddesses of unbelievable beauty who quickly explained their need (Plate 47). Now these goddesses seemed not to trust alone to their bodily charms to win the award. Juno promised to make him ruler of vast and rich kingdoms. Minerva promised him military victory against the hated Greeks. But Venus, understanding best a young man's heart, offered him the fairest woman in all the world. To Venus, then, he handed the golden apple.

The fairest woman in all the world was Helen, daughter of Zeus by the beautiful Leda. So many had sought the hand of Helen in marriage that it was agreed that once a decision had been reached and she had selected from the host of suitors one to be her husband, all the rest would pledge themselves to protect this fortunate individual against any future enemies. So the oaths were taken and the pledges made. Menelaus was chosen and won thus for himself a beautiful queen and the rich kingship of Sparta.

Venus directed Paris to the home of the happy couple, where he was hospitably received (Plate 48). But when Menelaus left on a journey, Paris exercised either strength or charm or perhaps a combination of both, and carried Helen off to Troy (Plate 49).

Menelaus prepared his forces to sail for Troy and reduce that hated city to ashes. A thousand ships were ready at Aulis, but no favorable winds did blow to speed them on their course. Calchas, the seer, then spoke up and announced that some goddess had been offended by Agamemnon, brother to Menelaus. A compensatory sacrifice, therefore, must be made.

It was decided that Iphigenia, daughter of Agamemnon who was to command the fleet, must be offered (Plate 50). This was a harsh demand on the brave leader of men, and all of Greece awaited his terrible decision. Agamemnon himself brought his daughter to the sacrificial altar.

Then the winds swung around in the sky and blew favorable, speeding ten hundred ships Troy-ward.

Now for nine long years, this futile war was waged and neither side had any great advantage. The Greeks then began to fight among themselves because Achilles was unwilling to give up Briseis, a beautiful young captive who had been earlier awarded to him (Plate 51). Achilles agreed sullenly to the forfeit, but announced that he would fight no longer in the war against Troy, being determined to return to Greece.

This was a war incidentally in which the gods and goddesses of Olympus took sides and many a battle was won through Olympian intervention. Juno and Minerva naturally fought against Troy and Paris. Apollo helped both sides, varying his support as the caprice of the moment dictated. Zeus remained for the most part impartial and aloof, although on occasion he too made his power felt.

After Achilles retired to his tent, the Trojans attacked and forced the Greeks back to the shores where their ships were anchored. Then the Greeks knew that they needed Achilles at the battlefront, and Ulysses and Ajax went to inform the great warrior that Agamemnon had at last consented to the return of Briseis. But Achilles was adamant. The Trojans were again successful in the next day's battle, and won their way to the shore and set fire to many of the Grecian ships. The fight raged and neither side seemed close to victory. Achilles still remained sulking in his tent. The closest and dearest friend of Achilles was his childhood companion, Patroclus. When Achilles learned that Patroclus had been slain by Hector, his rage was terrible to see.

Now Achilles hastened to the field seeking vengeance. When King Priam looked down from the city walls, he saw his forces driven back to the gates, which he ordered quickly opened. Hector alone would not pass through the gates and remained outside the city to meet his sworn enemy. With his family and many of the survivors watching from towers and battlements, the two great leaders finally met.

Achilles approached, terrible in his wrath, looking more like the great god Mars than like a mortal. Even brave Hector quailed at the sight of so terrible a foe. Then the Trojan threw his spear, and although well aimed, it could not pierce the armor of Achilles. It bounded back, leaving the Greek unharmed. Then Achilles aimed his spear and loosed it in a mighty throw. It found its mark and in an instant Hector lay dying on the ground.

As the horrified spectators looked on, this body

which but a moment before was so full of life, was stripped of all armor and lay naked and exposed in the dust (Plate 55). Achilles now took a strong rope and tied it to the feet of his vanquished foe. Then he fastened the cord to his chariot and mounting quickly, beat his horses and dragged the body of dead Hector back and forth before the city.

Then the once haughty king went to a soldier's tent and prostrated himself before Achilles and kissed those same hands which had slain and dishonored his loved one. Priam said, "Think at this moment of your own father and what would be his feelings if Achilles and not Hector lay thus dishonored in the dust." And Achilles looked at Priam's sad countenance and saw how white was his hair and he did think of his own father and his heart ached. Then he gave his hand to Priam and raised him to his feet and granted him the body of his favorite son.

At this point peace might have come for Greek and Trojan, for Achilles had seen and become enamored of Polyxena, daughter of King Priam. This happened during the period of truce allowed for Hector's burial. Achilles had visited the temple of Apollo to arrange for the marriage when Paris, never a brave man, saw the great warrior and without warning shot a poisoned arrow at him which pierced his heel, the only part of Achilles which was vulnerable. His mother had dipped him when he was an infant into the river Styx but had held him by the heel, which remained the only place where the waters could not work their magic.

The Trojan forces were now encamped within the city which seemed impregnable. Ulysses, however, finally thought of a way to bring the war to an end. He caused to be constructed a huge wooden horse which was hollow and capable of housing a band of armed men (Plate 53). On a dark night the Greeks wheeled the horse before the gates and pretended to have given up the war and set sail. They did indeed take to the ships and anchored only a short distance away in a sheltered cove invisible from Troy's towers. As Ulysses had foreseen, the Trojans planned to bring the horse through their gates. Only Laocoön, a priest of Neptune, warned against such a move, exclaiming, "I fear the Greeks even when they bear gifts."

While some might have heeded the priest, an event took place which affected the decision. Two huge serpents came out of the sea and writhed their way to where Laocoön stood with his two sons. The serpents wound their terrible bodies around the group and slowly strangled all life out of father and sons (Plate 54). This the Trojans interpreted as a sign from Olympus that the offering must be drawn into the city.

Amid great celebrations this was done. That night Ulysses and his men stole from the belly of the horse, overpowered the few guards and opened the city's gates. The Greek forces had meanwhile sailed back into port and in a few terrible hours the city was sacked and the long war for Helen was over.

ADVENTURES OF ULYSSES

Turner   National Gallery, London

POLYPHEMUS DERIDED BY ULYSSES

Ulysses addressed the Cyclops in mocking and boastful tones
(pp. 97, 101)

Plate 57

Dosso Dossi

Kress Collection, National Gallery of Art,
Washington, D. C.

CIRCE AND HER LOVERS

*All who ate at her table were transformed
into animals of various kinds (pp. 97, 102)*

Plate 58

Spranger   *Vienna Museum*

ULYSSES AND CIRCE

Circe became enamored of Ulysses (pp. 98, 103)

Plate 59

THE SIRENS
Ulysses ordered his men to fill their ears with wax, so that they would be deaf to the sirens' song (pp. 97, 104)

Plate 60

Burne-Jones
Holford Collection. London

ULYSSES AND NAUSICAÄ

Gleyre

Ulysses, now fed and clothed, appeared
like a hero and leader of men (pp. 98, 107)

Collection of A. M. de Clerq, France

Plate 61

Pompeian Fresco

ULYSSES IN THE LAND
OF THE LAESTRYGONIANS

*The mariners came to a land which was
the habitation of the Laestrygonians (pp. 98, 101)*

Plate 62

Raoux   *Louvre, Paris*

TELEMACHUS IN SEARCH
OF HIS FATHER

*It is said that while searching for his father
Telemachus came to the island of Calypso* (p. 98)

Plate 63

Pintoricchio   National Gallery, London

THE RETURN OF ULYSSES

*Penelope had waited patiently all this time refusing
to believe that her husband was dead (pp. 97, 108)*

Plate 64

CHAPTER X

THE ADVENTURES
OF ULYSSES

THE LITERARY source for this story of Ulysses is, of course, Homer's *Odyssey*. In this immortal work there are chronicled the many adventures of Odysseus (this is the Greek equivalent for Ulysses) after he sailed from Troy.

The story of Ulysses has naturally intrigued many artists. To illustrate this chapter I have selected paintings which vary in style, period and merit. I feel that not one of them is as noble as the text which served as inspiration. The classical world of Homer is seen through the temperaments of Italian, English and French painters of later centuries. Still we are afforded an opportunity to see how the Renaissance painter, Pintoricchio, imagined the "Return of Ulysses" (Plate 64). If it is not a true picture, it is still an enchanting one. We have a later Italian painter's version of "Circe and Her Lovers" (Plate 58). There is the Englishman Turner's melodramatic rendering of the ship of Ulysses threatened by Polyphemus, and also Burne-Jones' rather queer and insipid conception of the voyage past the Sirens (Plates 57, 60).

The remaining pictures are labeled to indicate subject matter and authorship. It will be evident that Homer's "word paintings" of the adventures of Ulysses still remain the most wonderful of all (Plates 59, 61, 62, 63).

Departure from Troy—The Lotus Eaters

The war for Troy was finally over and a great city lay in ashes. Its heroes were dead. Only Aeneas and a few of his followers succeeded in escaping from the burning town and a Greek army maddened by victory. On that terrible day much offense was given to the gods, for the conquerors forgot all humility and decency.

For evil such as this the victors were destined to pay. When the ships set sail, great storms arose, sent by Neptune. The fleet was scattered and many a Greek, so recently flushed with victory, sank forever in the black and angry sea. It was ordained that Ulysses would survive, but not before he had wandered for ten long years, far from Ithaca, his homeland, and his loved ones.

The great storm which arose and dispersed the Greek fleet lasted for nine days and when it subsided an island was sighted. It was the land of the Lotus, a plant which when eaten resulted in complete loss of memory. Ulysses managed to get his crew away from the strange island without too serious mishap.

The Cyclops Polyphemus

When the ship next put into port, it was in the land of the Cyclopes, a breed of giants, huge men with only one eye, which was placed in the middle of the forehead. These titans lived in caves and spent most of their time guarding the flocks off which they fed. Ulysses and some of his men began to explore the island. They happened on one of the caves, the home of the Cyclops Polyphemus. Ulysses and his followers were about to congratulate themselves on finding so rich a stock of food, when Polyphemus suddenly returned, driving a large flock before him. With greatest ease he then rolled an immense boulder in front of the cave's opening and Ulysses and his frightened men knew that all their concerted efforts would never move it. When Polyphemus had milked the goats and ewes he happened to roll his obscene eye around in its socket and saw that he had visitors. He asked them who they were and whence they came.

Ulysses stood up as spokesman and told of the Trojan War, and spoke with great humility and begged that he and his men might be received kindly. Polyphemus answered by grasping two of the men and throwing them against the cave wall and dashing out their brains. Then he tore them apart, limb by limb, and devoured them. Having supped so well, he lay down and fell into a deep and relaxed sleep. Ulysses would have attacked him but knew that if they did succeed in slaying the Cyclops, he and his men would be prisoners forever in the sealed cave. In the morning Polyphemus breakfasted off two more of the band, rolled the rock from the opening to allow himself and his flocks an exit, and then sealed it up again. When he was gone, the crafty Ulysses planned his revenge and escape. That evening the giant returned, and again killed and devoured two men. But before he could fall asleep, Ulysses and a group of his most daring followers approached the Cyclops and offered him a jug of wine which they had carried with them from the boat. Polyphemus tasted it and found it good. He announced that as a reward for this delicious drink, Ulysses would be the last to be eaten. "What is your name?" he inquired of the leader. "My name is Noman!" Ulysses replied.

While the Cyclops had been out with his flocks, Ulysses had a great log cut, tapered it at one end to a sharp point, and concealed it in the rear of the cave. When the one-eyed titan finally fell into a sleep deepened by the drinking of so much wine, the men heated the point of the log in a fire which they had made until it was hot and glowing like a burning coal. Then Ulysses lifted it and placed the point in the giant's single eye. The men jumped to his aid and they twisted the log until the eye was completely burned out of its socket.

A horrible scream of rage and pain filled the cave and the men ran to its corners to be out of reach of the blinded Cyclops. Hearing his cry, other Cyclopes came out of their caves and called to Polyphemus, "Who is it that hurts you?" The agonized giant answered, "Noman!" and the giants reasoned that if no man was harming Polyphemus this must be some divine visitation and they returned to their caves.

In the morning Polyphemus stood at the entrance to the cave and having rolled the stone away only far enough to let the cattle pass through, he felt each creature as it went by, to make sure that no human escaped. But Ulysses had ordered his men to guide the flock to the exit in groups of three abreast. Clinging to the under-side of each middle ram were the surviving members of the band. As soon as they had all escaped, Ulysses being the last, they rushed to their boat beached on the shore. Ulysses was not satisfied only to be safe. He now addressed the Cyclops in mocking and boastful tones. "O Polyphemus, if you would know who brought this just punishment upon you, it is I, Ulysses, sacker of cities, and to me alone you owe the loss of your monstrous eye!" (Plate 57)

The Laestrygonians

After several uneventful days at sea, the wanderers came to the island of Aeolus, who governed the winds. On their departure from the island, they ran into another great storm.

Finally, the mariners sighted a land which was the habitation of the Laestrygonians (Plate 62). Taking to small boats, they beached in a quiet cove. Only Ulysses remained off shore. The Laestrygonians, a fierce and warlike people, waited until the boats were anchored, and then attacked. Many vessels and many men never again sailed out of these quiet waters.

Circe

The survivors plied their oars and came next to the island of Circe, an enchantress and daughter of the Sun.

When they approached the island of Aeaea, Ulysses ordered a scouting party to investigate the land before the entire party disembarked. Now Circe, as has been mentioned, was a witch and an enchantress who lured men to her by her rare beauty. She entertained them lavishly and bade them sup with her, but once they had eaten of her fare, they were transformed into animals of various kinds, retaining only their human minds, but in all other respects being as the beasts of the fields and forests (Plate 58).

Eurylochus led the group of men toward a palace which was located in the center of the island. From within they heard the strains of sweet music and a woman's voice, lifted in song. When they called, Circe appeared and bade them welcome. Only Eurylochus, the leader, was suspicious, and remained outside. Circe conducted the men to an impressive banquet hall and served them with wines and tempting foods. But when they had eaten, she touched them one by one with her magic wand, and they were transformed into swine. Then the horrified Eurylochus hurried back to the ship to describe to Ulysses the fate of his men. When the story had been told, Ulysses determined to go alone and attempt single-handed the rescue of his shipmates.

On the way he met a youth of godlike beauty, who announced that he was Mercury and had come to aid Ulysses. He gave the Ithacan a special herb which, once he had eaten of it, would protect him from any harm.

Circe greeted Ulysses as she had greeted his men, and entertained him in the same rich manner. But when she touched him with her wand, no transformation took place. Instead, Ulysses drew his sword, rushed upon her and threatened to kill her unless she immediately released all her prisoners from their beastly shapes.

Then Circe, fearful for her life, restored all the men to their human forms. The rest of the company now came ashore, and a great celebration was held. Circe became enamored of Ulysses, and he and his companions found life on the island exceedingly good (Plate 59). Soon they had forgotten home, family, the horrors of the war and their many trials. But even with this attractive way of life, with its luxuries and pleasures, they found themselves finally surfeited. And the thoughts of the brave men turned once more to the sea and adventure.

Circe reluctantly helped with preparations for the journey and supplied the wanderers with food and supplies. She also warned them of dire perils which awaited them, but explained how to evade them.

The Sirens—Scylla and Charybdis

First there were the Sirens, a species of sea nymph, who could charm with their irresistible songs all mariners who sailed within earshot of their chants. It was said that sailors hearing the melodies would throw themselves into the sea in their mad desire to join the makers of such seductive melody. Ulysses ordered all his men to fill their ears with wax, so that they would be deaf to the Sirens' song (Plate 60). He then had his companions tie him to the mast, instructing them not to unbind the fetters no matter how he might plead to be free. When they sailed past the rocks where the Sirens dwelt, so alluring was the music which Ulysses alone could hear, that he almost broke his bonds. But his men heeded not his pleas or threats, and after a while, no further sound of singing carried across the water and Ulysses was unloosed from his bonds.

Circe had also warned that a grave danger awaited him when his course compelled sailing between the twin perils of Scylla and Charybdis. Scylla lived high on a stony promontory rising out of the sea. Being equipped with six heads on long necks, she could reach out towards a passing ship and diminish the crew by that number, devouring the helpless mariners in a manner awful to behold.

Close by lay the other danger, the whirlpool Charybdis, which sucked ships and all aboard into its churning depth. Although Ulysses had been forewarned and managed to steer away from the whirlpool, he could not successfully evade the bestial Scylla. The boat came just close enough to permit her to stretch out her serpentine necks and pluck six brave men from their places at the oars and lift them to her rocky perch, there to make her repast.

Calypso

After rowing and sailing for many days, the men sighted the island of the Sun God, where grazed the sacred flocks of Hyperion. The members of the crew were too famished to resist the temptation of slaughtering and eating some of the sacred animals. As soon as the voyage was continued, terrible punishment was exacted for this sacrilege. During a prodigious storm lightning struck the boat and shattered it. Every last man of the crew drowned that day, but Ulysses, clinging to the keel and mast, which he had lashed into a raft, finally floated ashore on the island of the sea nymph, Calypso.

This beautiful enchantress may have heard of Ulysses and the victory at Troy and therefore have come quickly to the aid of so great a hero. Or it may be that Ulysses was a man of such virile charm and attraction that, like Circe and other women, she immediately fell in love with him. But such were her own attractions, that this tired wanderer was tempted to remain forever on the seagirt isle. However, he could not completely put out of mind thoughts of his son, Telemachus, and memories of his dear wife, Penelope. Calypso, although earthbound, was related to the gods and goddesses of Olympus and promised her lover immortality if he remained with her. But in spite of her blandishments and feminine wiles, Ulysses gazed often across the seas, his sad countenance revealing that his thoughts were elsewhere. Then one day, Jupiter, feeling that Ulysses had done enough penance, ordered Mercury to take the message to Calypso that the Ithacan must be released.

Sorrowfully, the nymph conceded to this divine order, and helped Ulysses prepare a raft. She furnished him with ample provisions and one dawn when the sea was calm and the winds blew gently, he bade her farewell and began his last lonely voyage.

But once more was his soul to be tried. Again a storm arose and the raft was tossed high on angry waves and finally destroyed. Ulysses swam until exhausted and was washed ashore, helpless and close to unconsciousness, on the land of the Phaeacians.

Nausicaä and the Phaeacians

These people who inhabited the country of Scheria were a good, peace-loving and hospitable folk. Alcinoüs was the king, and he had a daughter, Nausicaä, who in anticipation of her imminent marriage, had gone with her companions to wash the robes of state at a clear spring not far from where Ulysses had floated ashore. When the princess and her friends had finished with their chores, they bathed their young bodies in the cool waters.

Ulysses was awakened by the girlish screams and laughter and realizing that he was naked and ill-kempt, he was fearful of appearing thus before these gentlewomen. Then he broke a leaf-covered branch from a nearby tree and holding it before him as a covering, he stepped from his hiding place. No sooner had they seen and heard him than they fled in fright, all but Nausicaä, who, instructed and made fearless by Minerva, listened as Ulysses told his story and made his plea for food and clothing. Then she recalled her friends, telling them that there was naught to fear, and soon Ulysses was fed and washed and clothed. Now he no longer appeared as a shipwrecked derelict, but truly as a hero and leader of men (Plate 61). Nausicaä, being a maid of good sense and some knowledge of the world, told Ulysses to remain behind a while and after the party had a good start, to make his way to the city alone, and appear then at the palace and appeal for help to her generous father, King Alcinoüs.

Ulysses did as she suggested and he told of his sojourn on Calypso's isle and of his ill fortune with the raft. He also related how generously their daughter, Nausicaä, had cared for him in his time of dire need.

The Return Home—The Fate of the Suitors

Alcinoüs then promised that Ulysses would be furnished with a ship and crew so that he might reach his native land.

The king and his courtiers lavished rich and varied gifts on the ill-fated wanderer and in the morning a crew of the bravest Phaeacians put to sea in a sturdy boat. Before they reached Ithaca, Ulysses fell into a peaceful sleep and the men lifted him and carried him ashore when land was reached and left him there on his own soil, surrounded by the many gifts and presents.

When Ulysses awakened, he was deeply puzzled, for it was twenty years since he had last trod the blessed earth of Ithaca, and he saw nowhere a familiar landmark. Suddenly his steadfast patron, Minerva, appeared to him. She told how Penelope had waited patiently all this time, refusing to believe that her husband was dead, and how she continued to hold off the band of pressing suitors who would not move out of the palace and were eating his food and drinking his wines. She explained that at that very moment, his good son, Telemachus, was traveling from place to place, making futile inquiries for his father. She added that a divine messenger had been sent to recall his son so that together they might plan their vengeance (Plate 64).

Eumaeus, the faithful servant of Ulysses, had refused, like Penelope and Telemachus, to believe that his master would not return; and Minerva led Ulysses to the old swineherd's hut, having first transformed him into the semblance of an old and ill-clothed itinerant beggar. Eumaeus none the less greeted him with kindness and proffered shelter and food.

When Telemachus returned, having evaded a death trap set for him by the conspirators, he found this strange old man in the company of his father's servant. He, too, greeted him kindly. Then Eumaeus left for the palace to tell Penelope of her son's safe return, and it was this interval which Minerva selected to transform Ulysses back to his true shape. Telemachus gazed in awe and wonderment at the godlike figure standing in his presence. Quickly the tale was told and father and son embraced, the tears wetting their cheeks. But Minerva warned that time was short and speedily the plans were laid. Ulysses again assumed his former shape of a defenseless old beggar, and in this disguise went to the palace to beg some charity of the celebrating revelers.

Penelope had meanwhile announced that a series of contests would be held to determine which aspirant should be her chosen groom to replace the noble Ulysses. She ordered Telemachus to bring the great bow of his father, which had hung unstrung and unused for twenty years. Twelve rings were now arranged in a continuing line, and he who could shoot an arrow through all twelve would have Penelope as the prize. Meanwhile, Telemachus had removed all other weapons from the room.

Now as each suitor stood up to make trial, not one among them could even bend the great bow to string it. When the humble beggar asked to be given a chance, the hall echoed with mocking laughter. But Telemachus insisted that the old man be handed the bow.

The assembled plotters now gasped in bewilderment when, with greatest ease, the scorned old man bent the bow and fitted the string to its notch. In an instant he had loosed an arrow and it winged swiftly through all the rings. Quickly, another arrow was fitted to the bow, but this one pierced the throat of the most arrogant of the suitors. Now all was panic. Telemachus and Eumaeus rushed to the support of a transformed Ulysses, noble once more in appearance, and flaming like a god. Arrows and spears found their marks with death-giving insistence. Blood flowed everywhere as corpse was heaped upon corpse. At last all were dead. Ulysses and his small loyal band gazed in awe at the havoc which they had wrought. But when he laid down his bloody weapons, this hero of wars and perilous adventures knew that at last he was master again of his own domain.

Artists Whose Works Are Reproduced in This Book ... Their Schools and Dates

ITALIAN SCHOOL

Benozzo Gozzoli	1420	1498
Pesellino	1422	1457
Antonio Pollaiuolo	c1429	1498
Giovanni Bellini	c1430	1516
Andrea Mantegna	1431	1506
Luca Signorelli	c1441	1523
Sandro Botticelli	1444	1510
Pintoricchio	c1454	1513
Piero di Cosimo	c1462	1521
Titian	c1477	1576
Dosso Dossi	c1479	1542
Raphael	1483	1520
Antonio A. Correggio	c1494	1534
Paolo Veronese	1528	1588
Guido Reni	1575	1642
Giovanni B. Tiepolo	1696	1770

ENGLISH SCHOOL

J. M. W. Turner	1775	1851
Edward Burne-Jones	1833	1898

FLEMISH SCHOOL

Bart. Spranger	1546	1625
Peter Paul Rubens	1577	1640
Jacob Jordaens	1593	1678
Anthony Van Dyck	1599	1641

FRENCH SCHOOL

Nicolas Poussin	1594	1665
Claude Lorrain	1600	1682
Jean Raoux	1677	1734
François Boucher	1703	1770
Jacques Louis David	1748	1825
Eugene Delacroix	1798	1863
Charles Gleyre	1807	1874

SPANISH SCHOOL

El Greco	c1541	1614

ROMAN PAINTING

This was done by an unknown master who finished his work before the year 79 A.D. when Vesuvius erupted.

Recommended Readings

EARLY SOURCES

The Iliad — Homer
The Odyssey — Homer } Modern Library and other editions

The Theogony, etc. (Translated by A. S. Way)
Hesiod — Macmillan and Co., Ltd.

The Complete Greek Drama 2 vol. (Trans. by Frank Justus Miller)
Oates and O'Neill — Random House

Heroides-Amores (Translated by Grant Showerman)
Ovid — Harvard Univ. Press

Recommended Readings—Cont.

The Golden Ass (Translated by W. Adlington, S. Gaselee)
        Apuleius   Harvard Univ. Press
Argonautica (Translated by R. C. Seaton)
        Apollonius Rhodius Heinemann
The Library, etc. (Translated by Sir J. G. Frazer)
        Apollodorus   Heinemann
Odes (Translated by Sir J. E. Sandys)
        Pindar   Harvard Univ. Press

MODERN WRITERS

Mythology   Edith Hamilton   Little, Brown
Heroic Tales from Greek Mythology
        Katherine Pyle   Lippincott
Bulfinch's Mythology
        Thomas Bulfinch   Modern Library
Gods and Heroes   Gustav Schwab   Pantheon
Classic Myths in English Literature and in Art
        Charles M. Gayley Ginn
Oxford Classical Dictionary   Oxford Univ. Press

MYTHOLOGY IN THE MODERN NOVEL

Hercules, My Shipmate
        Robert Graves   Creative Age Press

RECOMMENDED FOR CHILDREN

The Golden Fleece* Padraic Colum   Macmillan
Stories of the Gods and Heroes
        Sally Benson   Dial

---

* From: *The Golden Fleece and the Heroes Who Lived Before Achilles.*

RIGHT: *Circe and Her Lovers* [DETAIL], Dosso Dossi